America's
Best Loved
Wild Animals

Also by Madeline Angell

120 QUESTIONS AND ANSWERS ABOUT BIRDS

The Bobbs-Merrill Company, Inc. · Indianapolis/New York

America's
Best Loved
Wild Animals

by Madeline Angell

Illustrated by Larry Veeder

ISBN 0-672-52042-7
Library of Congress catalog card number 74-17691
Designed by Jacques Chazaud
Manufactured in the United States of America

First printing

89-977

To my father and the memory of my mother,
who taught me to love all wild creatures, and
to C. A. M. and the memory of Anna,
who always treated me as their own daughter.

Contents

Introduction

This is a book written for people who secretly believe they know a little bit about what it's like to be a wild animal. I suspect that many of us who feel this way enjoyed animal stories at an early age. Perhaps we have learned to observe animal life and to ponder on what we see and hear. Or we may have great curiosity and imagination about what it's like to live another's life, whether it be a human life or one of the lower animals.

Certain wild animals have a greater appeal for us than others. At some time during the process of growing up, most of us have identified with the cottontail rabbit. One probable reason for this is our sympathy for the underdog. Rabbits are almost always the pursued, seldom the pursuer. Possibly we have been influenced by our familiarity with Peter Cottontail and the lovable character this name brings to mind.

The gray squirrel, so often described as "bright-eyed and bushy-tailed," is another favorite. Almost every city park has its quota of gray squirrels who mooch food from the more tender-hearted humans wandering through that park.

How you regard such creatures as moles and badgers may depend partly on whether *The Wind in the Willows* is one of the books with which you are familiar. No fan of this book could possibly regard Mr. Mole with one-hundred-per-cent dislike, even if he *is* ugly looking and *does* have a nasty habit of ruining lawns.

Perhaps we're intrigued by the question of what it must be like to live underground in a maze of tunnels. In similar fashion, we may wonder what it is like to be a muskrat or a beaver, tucked away snug for the winter in a home with an underwater entrance.

Most of us don't have any greater opportunity to see a deer or a bighorn sheep in the wild than we do a muskrat or a badger. But the sight of a deer standing silently in the woods, regarding us with big, solemn eyes, is a thrill long remembered, and the motion of its body as it leaps with incredible ease over a fence is grace personified. The bighorn sheep has the fascination of the mysterious, living far from civilization, in remote areas that most of us visit only on an occasional vacation—if at all.

What about meat-eating animals such as wolves, bobcats, and bears? We may have formed an association of fear with these animals. However, we may also feel attracted to them, because we may notice a strong resemblance between the wolf and our pet dog, between the bobcat and our domestic kitty. The bear can be amusing as well as frightening. If some of the animals in this book are not on your "best loved" list now, perhaps they will be in time.

The questions and answers which follow are designed to give you some information about your favorite animals.

Not many of them are animals we could keep as pets. Their size, temperament, style of life, or means of defense make this difficult or impossible. They are wild animals, and must be appreciated for what they are. But there are so many fascinating, little-known facts about their capabilities and life styles that the more you learn about them, the more your admiration and fondness for them is sure to grow.

Although animals such as the dolphin and the sea otter are loved by many of us, they are marine animals. This book presents only land animals found within the boundaries of the United States.

So read and enjoy, and then, if you have the opportunity, study these animals firsthand in their natural settings.

America's
Best Loved
Wild Animals

Opossum

Why have so few people ever seen an opossum in the wild?

They hide during the daytime, and even at night, when they are active, they are very secretive creatures. They are found in the eastern half of the United States and along the West Coast. But they are scarce in the northern part of their range.

What two characteristics make the opossum
distinctive in this country?

Of all the animals found wild in the United States, this is the only one that can hang by its tail. It is also the only one that carries its young in a pouch.

Opossums belong to the marsupial order, one of the first groups of mammals to evolve. Probably the most well known marsupial is the kangaroo. Most of the marsupials in the world today live in Australia and nearby regions.

Is the opossum really stupid?

Opossums rate very low on the scale of animal intelligence. Their brain case is much smaller than that of most other mammals of similar size. They do not seem able to learn from experience. For example, even after being caught in traps several times, they may not learn to become wary of them.

How does the opossum defend itself?

Not by speed, you can be sure! A possum has a slow, awkward gait and can easily be outrun by a man or a dog. He may climb a tree to escape his assailant and wait there until the enemy is gone. Or he may hide under a brushpile, rock, or hollow log, or in a hole.

An opossum usually chooses a small tree to climb, out of which he often may be shaken. In this case, or if he is unable to reach a safe hiding place, he will "play possum," acting as if he were dead.

His enemies include men, dogs, owls, coyotes, wolves, and foxes.

Is playing possum a clever trick or a state of shock?

Apparently, it is a true state of shock. Pulse and heartbeat are slowed. The opossum lies on its side, limp as a piece of cloth, with its eyes closed and its tongue hanging out. Opossums in this condition have endured all kinds of

abuse without showing any kind of reaction. A possum comes out of this deathlike coma as abruptly as he entered it. This usually happens when the assailant leaves. But it can happen sooner, and when it does, the assailant may receive a nasty bite from some very sharp teeth.

How does the opossum carry leaves for nest-building?

The leaves are passed from mouth to front paws to back paws to a loop in the tail. When there are several mouthfuls of leaves contained in the loop of the tail, the possum carries the leaves to the nest.

The nest is usually located in a tree cavity, a crevice between rocks, a brushpile, a woodpile, or an underground burrow.

How do young opossums reach the mother's pouch?

It was once believed that the mother placed them in her

pouch. Now it is known that the young ones climb into the pouch by themselves immediately after birth. This is quite an amazing feat, because they are not yet fully developed when they are born.

The young ones pull themselves up the mother's abdomen and into the pouch by making a kind of swimming motion wtih the front feet. They are about the size of a large pea, and look more like embryos than infants.

Why are many baby opossums doomed to
die almost immediately after birth?

The mother has about twelve nipples, although the exact number varies with the individual. Frequently, eighteen young are born. Those infants that find a nipple will receive the nourishment they need. They hang on to the nipple for several weeks without letting go. The infants that do not find a nipple die of starvation.

How long do the young ones
stay in the mother's pouch?

A month after birth, the young ones begin to let go of the nipple occasionally and peek at the world outside their "nursery." When they are about seventy days old, they begin to climb about on their mother. It is not unusual to see a mother opossum with her young ones riding on her back or even hanging onto her legs. When they are between two and three months old, the young ones are weaned. Soon after that, they become independent of their mother.

Does the opossum hibernate?

No, but it doesn't like the cold, and it may stay in its den for several weeks at a time during severe winter weather. It comes out to search for food when forced to by hunger.

What does the opossum eat?

Nearly everything. He eats small mammals, fish, frogs, birds, eggs, vegetables, fruits, nuts, and insects. His favorite foods are chickens, eggs, persimmons, and pawpaws.

Mole

Are moles really blind?

At one time, naturalists believed that moles were blind. Their eyes are exceedingly tiny. They are hidden by fur and are sometimes covered with skin. However, a study of the mole's eye reveals that it has all the structures required for normal vision. Most experts now believe that all moles can distinguish light from dark, though few are able to see objects. The common and the Western mole do not see as well as the shrew mole, the star-nosed mole, or the hairy-tailed mole.

Are moles deaf?

Moles have no external ears, but they have inner ears and can hear. They react to loud sounds. Some moles have been taught to respond to human voices or the ringing of a bell. However, their sense of hearing is probably not very acute.

How does a mole try to escape if aboveground?

Instead of trying to run away, he starts to dig. The speed with which a mole can dig himself in is truly amazing.

How is the mole adapted for digging?

His broad front feet turn outward and are shovellike, with five oversized claws for digging. His shoulders are broad and powerful. The mole pushes through the earth like a person swimming the breaststroke. His short, velvety fur can be brushed forward or backward and so does not offer any resistance to the earth. The fur-covered eyes and the absence of external ears are also adaptations for digging.

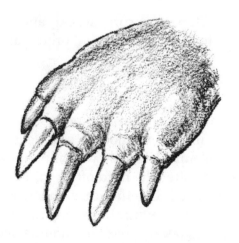

How does the mole turn around in his tunnel?
He slowly turns half a somersault.

Why do some tunnels have large hills
and others just a ridge of earth?
When he is hunting for food in soft earth, a mole may dig fairly close to the surface. He pushes the dirt up, form-ing the ridge that makes lawn owners so unhappy. To make the tunnel in which he will live, the mole must dig deeper, a foot or more beneath the surface. Then he has to push the dirt out of the entrance hole. This extra dirt creates the pile we call a molehill.

How does a mole catch his food?
He does most of his food-catching by enlarging tunnels he has dug before. As he enlarges these tunnels, the mole finds earthworms and insects and quickly gobbles them up. When he is digging a new tunnel, a mole eats as he goes along.

Do moles eat anything other than
earthworms and insects?
Yes. They sometimes eat corn, wheat, and oats. West-ern moles eat tulip and iris bulbs and other garden plants as well.

Do moles store food?
Apparently, American moles do not. European moles, however, have a unique method of storing food. When earthworms are plentiful, a mole will pile the "extras" in one spot. He either bites the head off or injures the worm by a bite near the head. In either case, the worm does not die; neither can it move until it regenerates the missing or injured part. This takes about two months. Meanwhile, the mole has a handy supply of fresh meat available.

Where are mole babies born?

In an underground nest that is lined with dried grass or leaves. If the nest is disturbed when the young are unable to care for themselves, the mother will carry them to another spot and make a new nest for them. After about a month, the young begin to leave the nest. They stay close to home for another few weeks.

How long do moles live?

Five years seems to be about the maximum age.

What enemies does the mole have?

If the mole is caught aboveground, a fox, skunk, or coyote may kill him. They don't seem to care for the musky odor, however, and may not eat a mole even after killing it. Hawks and owls not only kill moles, but eat them. Snakes sometimes follow them into their runways. Man kills moles when they disturb lawns, gardens, or golf courses.

Are moles useful in any way to man?

Yes. They eat from one-third to all of their weight in insects each day. Many of these are crop-destroying insects such as cutworms and Japanese beetles.

Although we don't like the ridges they make on our lawns, their tunnels do aerate the soil, which makes it more productive. In dry weather, rain water passes into mole tunnels and is thus conserved. In wet weather, the water that runs into the tunnels prevents the topsoil from becoming sour.

Cottontail Rabbit

*How can you tell a cottontail rabbit
from a jack rabbit and other hares?*

The ears and hind feet of a cottontail are noticeably shorter. The winter coat of a cottontail stays much the same color as his summer coat. The coat of a jack rabbit or a varying hare turns white in winter.

The white underside of the tail gives the cottontail its name. When it is hopping about, the rabbit raises its short tail, showing off the white "ball of cotton."

What is odd about the way a rabbit moves?

Most animals move about by walking or running. Cottontails and their close relatives move forward by hops and leaps. Cottontails can leap ten or fifteen feet at a time. Their top speed is about eighteen miles an hour, but they can't keep this up for very long.

Where are you apt to find cottontails?

Generally speaking, cottontails don't like dense forests, but you are apt to find them in any other place where there is food and shelter. They like thickets, brushpiles, brier patches, and fields where there is tall alfalfa, clover, or corn. They also like gardens and orchards, as we well know, and they prefer those that have tall grass, weeds, or brush along the edges, where they can hide.

When is the cottontail most active?

Cottontails get around both day and night. The most active times for them are the early morning hours, soon after sunrise, and the hours before and after sunset. Cottontails can often be seen on moonlit nights.

What is a rabbit "form"?

It is a place a rabbit uses for hiding or resting. The cottontail may scratch a shallow bowl for itself under a brushpile or in a brier patch. The form may be only a place where long grass has been trampled down in such a way that it leans over to form a "roof." Sometimes these forms are lined with fur, leaves, or grass. More often, they are not.

Rabbits usually have three or four such forms, with little paths connecting one to the other. Most have openings in the front and back. When the weather is bad, a cottontail seeks shelter in one of his forms and faces away from the wind.

In winter, rabbits prefer to find an abandoned burrow, a hollow log, a hole under roots, or some other well-protected spot. When the weather is severe, they can "hole up" here for a few days, not even venturing out for food.

*What kind of nest does the mother
cottontail make for her young?*

She digs a slight hollow in a field, meadow, lawn, or garden, and then lines it with grass and her own fur. Matting grass and more fur plucked from her breast, she makes a covering to put in place when she is gone. The nest is so skillfully concealed that it takes a sharp eye to discover it. We once had a cottontail nest right in the middle of a large expanse of lawn. Another was located in a flower bed next to the house.

There are usually from four to seven young born. The mother is gone from the nest during the day, but, as a rule, she stays close enough to defend her babies if they need her. At night, she removes the nest covering and nurses the young ones. They stay in the nest about two weeks. Soon afterward, they are weaned and on their own.

What do rabbits eat?

Rabbits are vegetarians. They eat almost any kind of grass or herb. Their favorite foods are clover and alfalfa. As any gardener knows, they like the vegetables we raise. (A tight chicken wire fence around the garden will keep them out.) They also eat the shoots, buds, leaves and bark of various shrubs and trees. In winter, they survive on dry grasses, evergreen plants, and bark. They don't have stored food to fall back on. Rabbits don't eat bulbs or tubers, although people sometimes blame them for this.

How do cottontails express emotion?

Baby rabbits give a squeal when they are alarmed and a scream when very hungry. Their mother may utter low grunts in conversing with them. On the whole, cottontails are very silent animals. They express both anger and fear by stamping their hind feet. Those who have heard the death scream of a rabbit say it resembles the cry of a human infant and is very distressing to hear.

What enemies does the cottontail have?

Just about every meat-eating mammal, bird, and reptile kills rabbits for food. The average life span of a cottontail is less than two years; the majority of them don't reach their first birthday. In years when there are fewer rabbits than usual, there is an increase in the number of other small animals killed by predators.

Rabbits would soon become extinct if they did not reproduce so fast. Each female has two, three, or even four litters a year. There are usually from three to six young in a litter.

How does a rabbit escape from its enemies?

Its main defense is to avoid being seen, either by "freezing" or by fleeing. Like a fox, a rabbit is clever at losing his pursuers. He doubles back on his track, jumps off to one side, and lets his pursuers pass by him. He may swim, in spite of the fact that he doesn't like water. If he can find a safe hiding place, such as a brushpile or the empty burrow of a woodchuck or badger, he will hide there.

Do rabbits really die of fright?

Yes. A number of cases have been recorded where a rabbit has died from shock. Apparently, the sound of gunshot or the realization that he cannot escape his pursuer is sometimes enough to kill a rabbit.

On the other hand, rabbits sometimes show great courage. Mother rabbits, defending their young, have been seen chasing snakes and hawks. In one case, it appears that a mother cottontail killed a skunk. Even after the skunk was dead, the rabbit was still squealing and kicking at it with her hind feet. This is the way a rabbit fights—by leaping over its opponents and kicking back with its hind feet. A rabbit can also give deep scratches with its sharp nails.

Woodchuck

*How can you tell if a woodchuck
burrow is being used by a woodchuck?*

It will have a large mound of dirt piled up near the
main entrance. Since a woodchuck cleans out the burrow
several times a week, it is likely that there will be fresh dirt
on the pile. There will also be tracks leading to and from
it, and it will give off a strong, musky odor.

If you watch such a mound over a period of time, you
should be able to see the woodchuck sunning himself or
using the mound as a lookout post.

Abandoned woodchuck holes are often claimed by other
animals such as rabbits, weasels, foxes, opossums, and
skunks.

How big is a woodchuck burrow?

It depends on how long it has been in use. It may be a short tunnel with just one chamber, or it may have a number of tunnel branches and chambers. If it has been in use for several years, it may be fifty feet long. The tunnel is about a foot wide near the main entrance, but it narrows to half that size farther down.

How does a woodchuck prevent its
bedroom from being flooded?

The bedroom is usually located above the lowest part of the main tunnel. Then, even if water floods the tunnel, the woodchuck will be snug and dry in its bedroom. The bedroom may be located just a couple of feet below the surface of the ground. The main tunnel may be four to six feet deep.

Does the woodchuck have special
spots he uses for a toilet?

Yes. There is usually a special room set aside for a toilet. Woodchucks clean up after themselves by burying the excrement. They also clean out the toilet room quite often by carrying the contents outdoors. A number of other animals that live underground also have toilet rooms.

When the weather is nice and there are no enemies about, woodchucks use the dirt mound near the front entrance for a toilet.

How does he make sure he doesn't
get trapped in his burrow?

He has more than one door. The escape entrances, or "plunge holes," do not have mounds of dirt near them because they are dug from inside the tunnel. These entrances are hidden by the surrounding vegetation. There may be several of them.

Do woodchucks defend a certain territory?

They don't allow other woodchucks in their burrow, even when danger threatens. Other than that, they don't defend a territory. Sometimes, a number of woodchucks will be feeding together or sunning themselves in a choice spot.

Do woodchucks hibernate?

Yes. Hibernation of the woodchuck is so complete that the hibernation of other animals is often compared to it. Four to six months, or even more, of a woodchuck's year is spent in hibernation. Breathing slows down to one breath every six minutes. Its pulse becomes very slow. Body temperature drops to as low as 38° F. The animal does not feel anything or hear anything. If moved to a warm room, he would take several hours to waken.

How does the woodchuck
prepare for hibernation?

First, he gets very fat. Some of this fat will be needed to carry on life processes during the winter. The rest will be used to tide him over during that period in early spring when food is scarce.

Then he plugs with earth the entrance to the chamber where he will be hibernating. This room, like the nesting chamber, is usually lined with dried grasses and leaves. A cottontail, skunk, or fox may take over the main living chamber while the woodchuck is having his winter sleep.

The woodchuck's final preparation is to roll himself into a ball with his head between his hind legs.

Is a woodchuck the same thing as a groundhog?

Yes. "Groundhog" is a popular name for the woodchuck. Very few people now believe, as did many in Colonial times, that if the groundhog sees his shadow on February 2, there will be another six weeks of winter. Actually, food is scarce when the woodchuck first comes out of his den in the spring, and that may well be the reason he decides to sleep awhile longer. However, that doesn't make him a weather prophet.

How long do woodchuck families stay together?

Only occasionally does the father stick around to care for the young. The young ones stay in the burrow with the mother, or close by, until they are six or seven weeks old. By the middle of summer, the mother insists that they leave her. The youngsters dig tunnels nearby. When fall comes, they usually go quite a distance away to dig themselves a winter den. They will not be fully grown until they are two years old.

What sounds do woodchucks make?

A woodchuck who is alarmed or who wishes to warn other members of the family gives a loud whistle or a twittering chirp. Several short chuckling notes may follow. Grinding of the teeth is another reaction to danger. During the mating season, the males fighting one another growl, snarl, and squeal. A low grunt or bark is used to express pleasure.

What do woodchucks eat?

Most of their diet consists of the leaves, flowers, and stems of various grasses and crops, such as alfalfa. They also like such delicacies as peas, corn, beans, melons, berries, and apples. In the spring, when other food is scarce, they may eat the bark and buds of trees. Only one per cent of their diets consists of insects. Farmers and gardeners sometimes find woodchucks a nuisance.

Prairie Dog

Why are prairie dog towns
so interesting to see?

Because there is so much activity to watch. Unless it is siesta time on a very hot day, there will be prairie dogs exploring the neighborhood, sitting on their haunches to look about, barking at an intruder, kissing one another, eating green vegetation, playing, grooming one another, working on their mounds, or popping in and out of their holes.

There are two main kinds of prairie dogs: the black-tailed, which live on the plains, and the white-tailed, which live in the mountains. The white-tailed are not so sociable as their plains relatives.

Where can you see prairie dog towns today?

Most of them are located in national parks or wildlife refuges. Some zoos have prairie dog towns. They are always a favorite attraction.

Prairie dogs were once very numerous, and some of their towns were enormous. An especially large one in Texas covered an area of 25,000 square miles and was estimated to contain 400 million inhabitants. Cattlemen killed off most of the prairie dogs with strychnine because the dogs competed with cattle for grass.

*How does a prairie dog burrow differ
from those of other animals?*

It has a listening post and a more vertical entrance tunnel. A short distance below the entrance, there is a small room dug to one side. This room serves as a listening post. When danger signals send a prairie dog diving into its burrow for safety, he may pause at this listening post instead of going all the way down to the nest chamber. If it turns out to be a false alarm, he'll soon pop back up again.

The entrance tunnel drops almost straight down—as much as sixteen feet—and then levels off. One or more grass-lined nest chambers branch upward from it after that.

*Why are there mounds of dirt around the entrance
to a prairie dog burrow?*

These mounds of dirt are like dikes. They prevent rain water from flooding the burrow. Some are very large; they may be ten feet in diameter and three feet high. When their mounds are damaged by rain or other causes, the prairie dogs repair them. They do so after a rain, when the earth is easily worked. Using their noses, they push the dirt into position and ram it repeatedly until it is tightly packed.

Why do prairie dogs cut down plants
they don't care to eat?

They do this as a safety measure. They don't want their enemies sneaking up on them in the shelter of tall weeds. So any plant in the area that gets to be over six inches tall is chopped down.

What other creatures often live in a prairie dog town?

It was once believed that rattlesnakes, burrowing owls, and prairie dogs all live peacefully together in a prairie dog town. Rattlesnakes frequently do take over an abandoned prairie dog burrow for a home. But their presence is not a welcome one, because they eat young prairie dogs. The same is true of burrowing owls. However, adult prairie dogs do not show much fear of the owls. Black-footed ferrets live in prairie dog towns and used to be the chief enemy. But ferrets are now so rare that they are on the endangered-species list. Rabbits, mice, and lizards also live in prairie dog towns.

What enemies do prairie dogs have?

Besides burrowing owls, snakes, and black-footed ferrets, prairie dogs fear badgers, coyotes, bobcats, ravens, hawks, and eagles.

What kind of signal system do prairie dogs have?

If one of them sees danger, he utters a high-pitched yip, which serves as an alarm call. In response to this, all other prairie dogs run to their mounds, bark, and look out for danger. If the danger is serious, each dives into his burrow. The "all clear" call comes when the emergency is over. The prairie dog stands on his hind legs and flings his forefeet in the air while giving this call; he may jump in the air or even fall over backward. Similar barks are used for greeting, friendly or otherwise. Some calls seem to be contagious; the whole town joins in the chorus.

How do prairie dogs greet one another?

There are various names for the greeting ceremony, but "kissing" seems to be as satisfactory as any. With mouths open, they touch their teeth together. Young prairie dogs make a habit of kissing all other prairie dogs.

Prairie dog towns are divided into sections, each inhabited by members of a clan. The kissing ceremony seems to be a ritual of identification. If a prairie dog is where he doesn't belong and is old enough to know better, the kissing is followed by a territorial bark. This means, "Go back where you belong." The other prairie dog seldom argues the point.

What is the life of a prairie dog pup like?

Prairie dogs stay in the burrow until they are six or seven weeks old. Then they follow the mother up the steep tunnel to the burrow entrance. Although the mother nurses the young when they are aboveground, the pups soon begin to nibble green plants and wean themselves. They play together and can often be seen grooming or kissing one another.

When the pups are completely weaned, the mother leaves them in charge of the old burrow and digs herself a new one, or finds an abandoned one. Soon after this, the youngsters leave the old burrow and dig themselves new ones.

What do prairie dogs eat?

Mostly grasses—such as buffalo grass and grama grass —and other plants. They also eat insects, particularly grasshoppers and beetles. Prairie dogs get along without much water, since they usually live in a dry climate. They drink water when it rains. At other times, they get moisture from the food they eat.

How do prairie dogs survive the winter?

Those that live on the plains get very fat and then retreat to their burrows when cold weather comes. They live off their accumulated fat, since they neither store food nor hibernate. In warm spells during the winter, they come out of their burrows to feed on roots and dry grasses that stick up through the snow. Those prairie dogs that live at high altitudes sleep through the winter.

How are prairie dogs able to withstand the glare of the sun?

Living as they do in treeless areas, prairie dogs are exposed to a lot of glaring sunshine. The orange-colored lenses in their eyes filter out some of this glare.

Chipmunk

How can you tell chipmunks
from other small mammals?

They are the only small mammals that have two light stripes on the sides of their faces. A dark stripe passes across the eye. They are also the only small mammals that have five dark stripes on the back and upper sides.

Where does the chipmunk spend the winter?

He digs himself a round or football-shaped burrow two feet or more underground. Beneath his bedroom, which is a foot in diameter or larger, he keeps his food supply.

At the beginning of the winter, there is so much food that there is barely room for the chipmunk to squeeze in on top. Between the chipmunk and his food supply, he makes a bed of dried leaves and grasses.

Some chipmunk burrows are simple, with just a tunnel and one living chamber. Others have a number of tunnels, living chambers, and storage rooms. There is usually a toilet room in these more elaborate burrows. Use of a special toilet chamber keeps the nest and storage areas clean.

When a chipmunk is digging, what does he do with the dirt?

He pushes it out with his nose, using one paw on each side of the nose to create a wider pushing surface. When a pile has accumulated, he either pushes it into the brush some distance away or plugs up the entrance and makes a new door somewhere else. The chipmunk is apparently smart enough to know that a pile of dirt at his front door would give his enemies a clue as to where they might find a meal.

Do chipmunks hibernate?

They don't hibernate throughout the whole winter as a woodchuck does. But in the north, they become cold and sluggish, in a state of hibernation, for days at a time. During most of the winter, they just sleep, waking up whenever they are hungry. Then they reach under the bed for some of their stored food. Occasionally, on a warm winter day, they will come aboveground to take a look around.

What kind of food does the chipmunk store for the winter?

He stores various kinds of nuts—acorns, hickory nuts, chestnuts, beechnuts, walnuts, peanuts, if he can find them. He transports food from the place where it is found to his burrow by filling his cheek pouches. He also stocks up on many kinds of seeds, such as seeds from pine cones, sunflower seeds, and maple seeds. He won't turn down a chance to put in a supply of corn kernels, wheat or rye grains, dry berries, flower bulbs, or corms. Whenever he finds more food than he can eat, he stores it, even if winter is still weeks away.

Chipmunks are noted for the large quantity of food they store. One chipmunk is on record as having stashed away a bushel of food in three days.

What do chipmunks eat in summer?

They like berries and fruits such as gooseberries, partridgeberries, wintergreen berries, strawberries, raspberries, blueberries, and wild cherries. Occasionally they will eat worms, june bugs, ants, beetles, snails, and birds' eggs. They have been known to eat field mice, young birds, frogs, and small snakes. In general, though, they are vegetarians.

Chipmunks often grow tame enough to take food from people and may become very fussy about what they will accept. One saucy little fellow who begged from me happened to discover that chocolate-covered peanuts were his favorite food. From then on, he would settle for nothing less.

Why are chipmunks seldom seen in hot weather?

When it's really hot, the chipmunk prefers to stay underground in his cool burrow. He comes out only if he runs out of food.

Do chipmunks sing?

You could say that they do. In addition to a warning "chuck-chuck" and an alarmed "chip-chip," the chipmunk has a "kuk-kuk" that is uttered softly. This is a musical sound that is continuous for anywhere from a few minutes to half an hour. It is quite a contented and sociable sound, and is sometimes referred to as a "song."

Does the father help care for the young?

No. The young are born in the nesting chamber in April. There are usually four or five of them, cared for solely by the mother.

How long do chipmunk babies stay in their underground birthplace?

About six weeks after they are born, the chipmunk youngsters venture aboveground. By the time they emerge into the warmth of the spring sunshine, they are about two-thirds the size of their mother.

When do young chipmunks know it is time to search for a new home?

When the mother thinks the young ones are big enough to fend for themselves, she chases them away. This is usually about two to three months after they are born.

What enemies does the chipmunk have?

Snakes and weasels are especially dangerous enemies because they can slither down into the chipmunk tunnel. Hawks, owls, mink, foxes, bobcats, domestic cats, and .22 rifles all play parts in reducing the chipmunk population.

How long do chipmunks live?

In the wild, they live an average of three to five years.

Gray Squirrel

What kind of home do gray squirrels have?

In winter, squirrels prefer a nest in the hollow of a tree. If they are unable to find one, they will build a nest of leaves high in a tree. You can tell a squirrel nest from a bird nest because the squirrel nest is rounded on top, not flat, as a bird nest is. It is waterproof and has an inconspicuous side opening.

We once raised two orphaned squirrels until they were old enough to care for themselves. They were about six weeks old when we got them. Their fur was not bushy and their tails were ratlike, but their eyes were open. We placed them in a cardboard box at first, then transferred them to a hamster cage. When they reached the point

27

where they needed more exercise than they could get in their confined quarters, we gave them freedom, several times a day, to run about in a room our children had used as a playroom.

In the cage, we kept a bit of soft, clean flannel. It was interesting to watch them cover themselves up at night, just as a child might do. The one we called Sookie, a personality-plus youngster, was very particular about the arrangement of his covers. He would snuggle close to his brother, then reach up with his little paws and pull the flannel over him until he was completely covered, head and all. During this whole process, he made soft scolding sounds.

Soon after we released the two squirrels into the yard, they built themselves a nest of twigs and leaves. It was high in the crotch of an oak tree close to the house. Alas, they were not very experienced. The nest lasted a few weeks, then came apart one night in a heavy windstorm. This is a fairly common happening; young squirrels are not expert nest builders. But by the time this nest collapsed, our squirrels knew the area well enough to find themselves a cavity in one of the trees in the wooded area beyond the house.

*Do squirrels defend a certain
territory as birds do?*

In some ways, squirrels are quite sociable. But they don't take kindly to strange squirrels in the neighborhood. A mother with young ones is especially possessive about the boundaries of her territory. When we released our two young squirrels into the yard, we were dismayed to find that they were continually engaged in fights. The other gray squirrels in the neighborhood regarded these two young ones as intruders and tried to drive them away.

Several times a day, our attention would be attracted by noisy chattering and squeals. Looking up, we would see one of our pets being chased from limb to limb by a furious attacker. A brief fight would be followed by squeals from the injured. There would be a leap through the air to another tree—first the pursued and then the pursuer. The fury of the fight would cause a shower of bark beneath the battle area. Then, after several short encounters, a great deal of chasing and being chased, and a lot of vocal comment, the loser would go far enough away to satisfy the victor. The victor would remain crouched on a tree limb, vigorously flicking his tail and still clucking away in righteous indignation.

Fortunately, our pets were strong and healthy, and although they lost most of their battles at first, they never gave up claiming our yard as their home. (Small wonder, since they came to us for food each day.)

Gradually, the other squirrels in the neighborhood accepted our pets as belonging. It was easier now to recognize Sookie from a distance. He had lost the tip of his tail in one of his battles. He and Scooter, his brother, grew more confident as they grew older and larger. By the end of the summer, they were refusing to allow other squirrels to use the feeding shelf we had built on the oak nearest the house. They squabbled some between themselves, but there were times when they sat side by side on the feeding shelf, each engrossed in eating faster, and therefore more, than the other.

Does the father squirrel help raise the family?

No. The father has several mates and does not take any part in caring for the young. The young sometimes stay with the mother as a family unit during the first winter.

How do young squirrels play?

While they lived with us, our two pet squirrels enjoyed wrestling with each other, climbing over us, and nibbling gently at our fingers and ears. Their favorite play equipment during exercise time was a webbed lawn chair. They scampered under and over the webs, obviously enjoying themselves.

One day Sookie found a key chain, and, holding it between his paws, he began to nibble it gleefully. Scooter was envious and tried to get it away from him. This made the key chain all the more valuable. Sookie would snarl a warning at Scooter, then turn his back to him and continue nibbling. Only when Sookie was tired of playing with it did Scooter have his chance, and by then Scooter had lost interest.

A few weeks after our pets had been running free in the yard, I sat on the ground and coaxed Sookie into my lap. He ran around me several times, leaped into my lap, turned over on his back, nibbled my fingers without hurting them, then leaped to the ground again. He repeated this performance several times, and then, catching sight of a dog headed in our direction, he took to a tree.

Occasionally you will see a squirrel dashing about on the ground as if he'd lost his wits. Instead of running in a circle, the ones I have observed have run in a triangle, with a somersault thrown in now and then for good measure. Apparently this is done in an excess of high spirits, since it is most apt to happen on a fine spring day.

The play of squirrels, like that of other animals, is part fun, part preparation for more serious adult activities.

Do squirrels learn from one another?

Yes. They observe one another and imitate those actions that appear to be successful. Watching our pet squirrels come to me for food, the other squirrels in the neighborhood decided they were missing out on a good deal. Soon I had a dozen or more squirrels coming to eat from my hand. Since Minnesota winters are harsh, I decided to make things easier for myself by leaving the storm sash off one kitchen window and placing a stepladder beneath it. Our pets quickly learned to climb to the top of the ladder and sit there until they had satisfied their craving for peanuts, which I passed out to them. Soon all the other squirrels in the neighborhood were doing the same thing. The feeding from the window had to be discontinued the following summer, however, when storm windows were replaced by screens. The squirrels born that spring imitated their elders but lacked the good manners of their parents. If I didn't happen to be right there when they arrived, they would clamber all over the screens; in their impatience, they soon began to chew at them. So, reluctantly, I had to remove the ladder.

What do squirrels eat?

In the spring, they nibble on tree buds and oak catkins. Occasionally they will take a young bird from the nest, and when this happens, you will see a squirrel being dive-bombed by the parent birds. But usually, squirrels are vegetarians, eating various kinds of nuts, fruit, berries, and large seeds. As you probably know, they also like bread crumbs.

I also discovered, while Sookie and Scooter were living in the house, that squirrels think the flowers of an African violet are delicious.

How do squirrels find the nuts they bury?

They can remember for only twenty minutes where they have buried the nuts. Fortunately, they don't need to rely on memory. Their keen sense of smell enables them to locate their store of food, even when it is beneath the snow.

*Do squirrels ever get killed walking
along electric wires?*

Yes. Occasionally they short-circuit the wires and are killed by the electric shock.

What enemies do gray squirrels have?

Gray squirrels are not often killed by other animals, because they are so alert, living in trees, and are active in the daytime, while most of their enemies are out and around at night. Foxes, coyotes, bobcats, hawks, owls, domestic cats, and man are the chief enemies of squirrels. Raccoons and snakes feed on young squirrels found in the nest.

Red squirrels will not tolerate gray squirrels in the same area. Although they are smaller, red squirrels apparently are better fighters; a battle usually ends with the retreat of the gray squirrel. It is not true that the red squirrel emasculates the gray one when they are fighting. There are seldom any serious injuries.

Do squirrels hibernate?

No. During a cold spell, squirrels may stay in their dens for a few days, eating from the supply of nuts and seeds they have stored there. But when milder weather returns, they will be out again, looking for food or sunning themselves in a wind-sheltered spot.

Do squirrels travel in large numbers?

In Colonial days, there were huge migrations of gray squirrels. Even now, although gray squirrels are much less plentiful, mass migrations sometimes occur. People become aware of this when they see a number of squirrels crossing a river, or moving through the woods by the hundreds. These migrations seem to happen when the squirrel population is up and the food supply is down.

Is a squirrel's tail useful?

Yes. When he is cold, a gray squirrel curls his bushy tail over his back for warmth. If he is hot, his tail provides shade. When he is climbing, jumping, or running along a branch, it helps him balance. If he falls, it acts as a parachute to slow his descent. If he must swim, it acts as a rudder. He expresses emotion with flicks of the tail. When a baby squirrel is being carried by his mother, he wraps his tail around her neck.

How long do gray squirrels live?

A number of squirrels kept as pets have lived to be fifteen years old. In the wild, they are not apt to live longer than ten years.

Red Squirrel

*How does the red squirrel compare
with the gray?*

Their names describe the difference in color. Reds are smaller and have a prominent white eye ring. The tail of the gray is bushier.

Like the gray, the red squirrel prefers to nest in a hollow tree but will build a nest of leaves if no tree cavity is available. Unlike the gray, the red squirrel will sometimes dig a burrow for a nesting site. This will probably be located under a tree or a stump. The family lives of the two squirrels are similar, and their enemies are much the same. Neither one hibernates, but they both hole up in bad weather.

Red squirrels prefer evergreen forests, and gray squirrels are more apt to be found where there are oak, beech, and hickory trees.

Why are red squirrels called
"sentinels of the forest"?

Like the blue jay, the red squirrel is a self-appointed news reporter. If anything unusual is going on in his territory, he spreads the word by his loud chattering and scolding. Even animals as large as the moose pay attention to his warnings. His nicknames—"chickaree," "barking squirrel," and "boomer"—come from the various sounds that he makes.

I watched a red squirrel the other day as he spread an alarm. He was leaning out over a branch, eyeing something on the ground. It seemed impossible that so much noise was coming from such a small animal. His high-pitched staccato chatter was interspersed with barks that were given with such gusto that he jerked forward with each one. All the while, he switched his tail back and forth spasmodically and stamped his feet so hard and fast that his body appeared to be shivering. As his excitement wore off a bit, his bark began to go up and down the scale and became softer, almost musical.

When I came to stand directly underneath him, he continued his monologue, glancing at me now and then as if to observe my reaction. Gradually he tapered off into silence. I could not help but think he had been enjoying his burst of self-expression.

Do red squirrels frequently rob bird nests?

Individual red squirrels seem to acquire a taste for eggs. There have also been reports of their eating young birds, young gray squirrels, and baby rabbits. But, in general, red squirrels are content to be vegetarians. Nuts and seeds from cones are their primary foods. They do not deserve the bad reputation earned for them by a few individuals. They perform a valuable service in the forests, because many of the pine cones they bury remain in the ground and eventually become pine trees. Besides, they are colorful, saucy little creatures, bursting with exuberance, fascinating to watch. There are people who feel that all red squirrels should be shot on sight. Naturalists do not agree.

Why do red squirrels cut pine cones off the tree before they are ripe?

This is very clever strategy on the part of the red squirrel. If he were to wait until the pine cones were dry and mature, the seeds would already be scattered. But when the cones are harvested in late summer, before they are ripe, the seeds are still locked inside by the pine scales. So the red squirrel gets very busy in late summer and early autumn. He climbs high in a tree and bites off the cones, which are fully grown but still green. After he has dropped a number of cones to the ground, he comes down the tree and shucks them, or carries them away to where he wants them.

Where does the red squirrel store his food?

The red squirrel who lives in our yard has piles of cones stashed away at the bases of several Scotch pines. He moves them about in stages. One afternoon in February, I watched him transfer cones from a pine tree about sixty feet away from the house to the woodpile where he lives. He made about a hundred trips back and forth. Investigating later, I found a stack of pine cones on top of the woodpile, where I had observed him depositing them. But two days after that, the cones had been transferred from the top of the woodpile to a spot hidden within it.

Sometimes red squirrels store their food in holes in the ground, or under rocks or fallen trees. Mushrooms, of which they are very fond, may be stored in the crotch of a tree or under loose bark. Red squirrels are able to eat mushrooms poisonous enough to kill a human.

A red squirrel's large pile of cones is called a "midden." This can be as large as thirty feet across. Underneath is the litter from the cones of previous years; on top is the current year's harvest.

Can red squirrels swim?

They don't like to swim, but they can. They have been known to swim across lakes seven miles wide and across rivers with strong currents. While in the water, they are in danger of being eaten by a large pike or a gull. Apparently, swimming is a great effort for them, because, in several cases, they have climbed up on canoe paddles and rested there before taking to the water again.

How does the red squirrel protect
itself against martens?

The marten is the red squirrel's most dangerous enemy. He can chase the squirrel through the tree and into the nest. The squirrel goes out on branch tips too small to support the marten's greater weight, then leaps to another slender branch. The squirrel's leaf nest is built with the marten in mind. Opposite the entrance is a spot where the wall is very thin. This is used as an emergency exit if the need arises.

What happens when a red squirrel
falls from a tree?

Occasionally a red squirrel will leap from a branch too unsteady to give him a good send-off and will miss the branch on which he has intended to land. To break his fall, he twists in the air until he is horizontal, spreads his legs wide, and stretches his tail out behind. This slows his fall. One red squirrel is known to have survived a fall of 140 feet without apparent injury.

How long do red squirrels live?

They can live to be ten years old, but very few of them do.

Flying Squirrel

Can flying squirrels really fly?

No. They glide. Loose, fur-covered folds of skin stretch from their wrists to their ankles. In the air, they spread their feet out to each side. Then these folds of skin open and act like sails. Air pressure from underneath forces the skin fold upward a bit, so that it resembles a shallow parachute. Although flying squirrels usually glide only about twenty or thirty feet, they can glide downward 150 feet at a time.

*How does a flying squirrel
prepare for its glide?*

It climbs high enough in a tree so that it can glide downward to its destination. Then it rocks from side to side several times. Apparently this is necessary for an accurate lining up of the distance and angle it intends to glide. If startled, it will glide without doing this, and then it does not always land safely.

How is the glide controlled?

By pulling down the left or the right "wing" just a bit, the flying squirrel can alter the direction of his glide. For example, pulling down on the right side will turn the creature to the right. He also controls direction and speed by moving his tail up, down, or sideways.

How does a flying squirrel slow down when it is landing?

It swings its tail and its body upward. This exerts a braking action. It lands against the tree with a soft thud, hind feet first, head up.

Why do people seldom see flying squirrels?

They are creatures of the night. Only if they are disturbed, as by having someone pound on the hollow tree in which they are nesting, will they appear during the daytime. If you want to catch sight of one, try flooding a bird feeder with sudden light at night.

What kinds of nests do flying squirrels prefer?

They like to build their nests in dead trees or stumps, bird houses, attics, farm buildings. Best of all is an empty woodpecker hole. Once in a while, they will settle in the abandoned nest of a bird or a gray squirrel. They line their nests with shredded bark, feathers, fur, dried leaves, or moss.

How long do the young stay with their mother?

Usually about a year. There is an average of four young in a litter. Like many animal mothers, the female flying squirrel won't allow the father near the nest while the babies are young. But when the offspring are well developed, the father sometimes moves back into the nest with the family.

Flying squirrels stay in their nests when winter weather is severe but come out to eat tree buds or buried nuts when the weather becomes milder.

What are the chief enemies of flying squirrels?

Owls and domestic cats are their worst enemies. Other nighttime creatures that prey on flying squirrels are raccoons, weasels, bobcats, and tree-climbing snakes.

Are flying squirrels "loners" as red squirrels are?

No. Flying squirrels like to be together with others of their kind. Sometimes the group is a family consisting of a mother and three or four of her young. Groups of twelve to twenty flying squirrels have frequently been reported, and one group in a hollow tree had fifty members.

They are gentle in disposition and make lovable pets. They are "night owls," however, and dislike being disturbed in the daytime. They must be handled very gently, since they are easily killed by too much pressure on the body.

Pocket Gopher

Why is there some confusion
over the name "gopher"?

The term "gopher" is sometimes incorrectly used to describe the thirteen-lined ground squirrel. Pocket gophers are unstriped. Their color may vary from nearly white to nearly black, but they are usually brown, about the color of the earth in which they live.

What is odd about a gopher's front teeth?

When the gopher closes his lips, his front teeth are on the outside rather than the inside. This allows him to use his upper front teeth like a shovel for digging dirt and keeps the dirt out of his mouth.

What is unusual about a gopher's cheek pouches?

They are lined with fur. Located under the skin, they extend backward from the mouth all the way to the shoulders. They are used for carrying food. He stuffs food into them with his front paws. When he wishes to empty them, he does so by running his front paws along his cheeks, from back to front.

Does a pocket gopher ever use his
cheek pouches for carrying dirt?

No, though many people believe he does. A gopher digs with his front teeth and his large front claws. He pushes the dirt out between his hind legs, which are spread far apart. Then he gives the dirt another push with his hind legs. When quite a bit has accumulated, he turns around with a somersault and pushes the dirt out to the surface through a side tunnel. He uses his nose and front feet for this final shove to the ground surface.

Is the gopher's tail of any use?

Yes. The tail, which is nearly hairless, serves as an organ of feeling. When the gopher is going backward in the tunnel, the nerve endings on his tail help him to know where he is. He can run backward as fast and easily as he can go forward.

Do gophers store food?

Yes. Their storehouses are blind alleys off the main tunnel. There are usually several of them. The gopher has a habit of storing more food than he can eat, and, as a result, some of it usually spoils.

How can you tell if there are gophers in an area?

It would be nice if it weren't so easy! Where there is a gopher, there will be numerous fan-shaped mounds of earth piled up above his tunnel. This earth comes from the

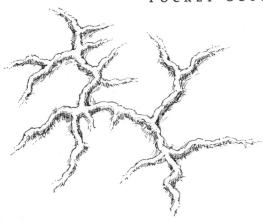

main tunnel. The gopher makes short, sloping side tunnels to the surface in order to get rid of the dirt. The mounds piled up by a gopher contain dirt that is more pulverized than dirt piled up by moles. They also contain earthen plugs, which mole mounds do not.

In the spring, after the snow has melted, you can often see where gophers have tunneled under the snow. Dirt from their belowground tunnels is sometimes shoved up into these under-the-snow tunnels. This dirt remains in the spring, evidence of winter gopher activity.

When do gophers work?

Day and night, in all seasons, with a little rest every couple of hours. They are such efficient diggers that not even the mole can match them. The burrows of one gopher may cover an acre of ground.

Is it true that gophers don't drink water?

Most gophers never drink water. They obtain the liquid they need from the green vegetation they eat. They are almost exclusively vegetarian.

Are gophers sociable?

They are about as unsociable as an animal can be. Except during mating season, adult gophers either will have nothing to do with one another, or they will fight until one is killed.

Young gophers are weaned when they are about six weeks old. By this time they are half-grown. They leave the home burrow soon afterward. Each one digs a burrow of his own and lives in solitude until mating season rolls around.

Do gophers keep a neat burrow?

Yes. They have a separate toilet room, and when it is full, they seal it off from the main burrow with dirt. They spend a great deal of time keeping their tunnels and rooms in good condition.

What natural enemies does the gopher have?

Owls, hawks, foxes, coyotes, wolves, and house cats snatch them up when they poke their noses out of their holes. Badgers, which can dig faster, go into the ground after them. Snakes sometimes manage to get in through a loosely plugged tunnel.

Why are gophers such a nuisance?

They eat grass, grain, fleshy roots of fruit trees, and stems and roots of such plants as alfalfa and potatoes. They get most of their food from underneath the ground, although they do come aboveground at times. They not only eat plant roots but often pull the stems into the tunnel from underneath. What is left of the plant aboveground withers and dies. As a result, they damage lawns, gardens, cultivated fields, pastures, and trees.

The mounds of dirt gophers raise are unsightly, and they make harvesting crops difficult. Their burrowing damages earthen dams and irrigation ditches.

In wilderness areas, gophers perform a valuable service by bringing up subsoil and aerating the earth.

Beaver

What is unusual about a beaver's growth?

Beavers never stop growing. Their rate of growth is slow, however, and most beavers in the wild live less than twelve years; this keeps them from growing to monstrous sizes. One captive beaver lived to be twenty.

How large do beavers get?

The record is held by a beaver that weighed 110 pounds. In general, though, beavers seldom weigh more than seventy pounds. The average beaver weighs from forty to sixty pounds, and is from three to four feet long, including the tail.

Why is the loss of a tooth
such a serious matter for a beaver?

The large incisor teeth a beaver has in the front of its mouth grow throughout its life. If one of these teeth is lost, death may result. The tooth opposite the lost one keeps growing. With nothing to grind it down, it grows in an arc until the beaver is no longer able to eat and so dies of starvation. Or the tooth may grow until it reaches the brain, causing death. This situation is true for other rodents as well.

Does a beaver use his tail as a
trowel to press mud into place?

A beaver's tail has many uses, but this isn't one of them. It serves as a rudder. When a beaver is towing a branch in the water, the weight of the branch has a tendency to make the beaver veer to the left or right, causing him to swim in a circle. To offset this, he turns his tail in the opposite direction. The tail aids him when he dives. It is used as a prop when he is sitting or walking on his hind legs. It is also used to slap the water as a warning signal that danger is near.

How does the beaver comb his fur?

There are special nails on his hind feet for this purpose. They are split in two. Beavers comb their fur to get out the tangles and to rid themselves of lice and fleas. The split toenails are also sometimes used to remove splinters caught in the teeth.

How does the beaver use his
front paws when swimming?

He doesn't! The hind feet and sometimes the tail are used to provide the necessary forward thrust. The beaver's front paws are folded neatly against his chest as he swims.

How long can a beaver stay underwater?

About fifteen minutes. There has been a good deal of research done in order to find out how an air-breathing animal manages to exist underwater so long. The beaver has valves which keep water out of his ears and nose when he swims underwater. He takes in much more fresh oxygen when he breathes than humans do. He has extra-large lungs. An oversized liver allows him to store a great amount of oxygenated blood. He has a greater tolerance than most animals for carbon dioxide, which builds up in the body when the breath is held.

What do beavers eat?

In winter, they eat the bark from branches and logs they have stored underwater near the lodge entrance. These have been fastened in place by sticking them into mud or piling stones on top of them. Poplar and aspen are their favorite trees. The rest of the year, they supplement their diet with various types of vegetation, such as lily pads and roots, marsh grasses, cattails, duckweed, and raspberry canes.

Why do beavers build dams?

They need to be sure the water in a stream or pond will be at least two to three feet deep. This depth of water protects them from their enemies and assures them of a safe place to store their food. Beavers don't have many enemies, other than man. In the water, they are usually safe, although an otter occasionally may kill a beaver. If caught on land, they may provide a meal for such animals as the wolf, coyote, bear, or bobcat.

*How do beavers make sticks stay in
place when they are building a dam?*

They place the sticks parallel with the stream's current and anchor them at one end with mud or stones. As more and more brushwood is laid in place, the branches interlace. This gives strength to the dam. Leaks are plugged with mud dredged up from the bottom.

When looking at a stump, how can you
tell if the tree was cut down by a beaver?

A beaver normally gnaws all around the base of a tree until the tree falls of its own weight. As a result, the stump will usually be cone-shaped, higher in the middle than on the sides. It also retains the chisel-like markings of the beaver's teeth. There will be many wood chips lying around.

How large a tree can a beaver cut down?

Most of the trees beavers cut down are from three to eight inches in diameter. However, beavers are on record as having cut down a tree that was five feet seven inches in diameter. They usually work alone to take down a tree, but once in a while two beavers will work together. When the tree is ready to fall, the beaver cutting it dives into the water, if water is nearby.

What happens to the tree after a
beaver has cut it down?

The family gathers round to eat the bark and remove branches from the trunk. They cut the branches into smaller pieces so they are easier to carry in the water. The larger sticks are used in the construction of a lodge or a dam. The smaller ones are stored near the lodge for food.

The tree trunk itself is cut into sections from two to eight feet long. As a rule, beavers do not attempt to move sections of the tree that are more than six inches in diameter.

Is it true that a beaver can always make
a tree fall toward the water?

No, although at one time this was the general belief.

Actually, the trees that a beaver topples near the water usually *do* fall toward the water. This is because the open side of a tree gets more sunshine, has more branches, and is therefore heavier. The tree leans in that direction and so falls toward the water. But when the beaver begins to take down trees farther away from the pond or stream, the trees fall every which way.

How do beavers move sticks and logs?

Sticks are carried in the teeth. Logs are rolled and pushed into place by one or two beavers. A beaver will use its teeth, feet, shoulders, and hips to move the log from the spot where it was felled to the water.

In the backwaters of the Mississippi, I have seen many "beaver runs." These are small canals dug by a beaver. They connect the area where beavers have been logging to the lake or slough where their lodge is located. Canals are used because it is much easier to move a log in water than it is to roll it over land.

How is a beaver lodge built?

The lodge is built along the shore, on an island, or in shallow water. If it is in shallow water, the beavers first build a foundation, sometimes using an upturned root, a rock, or a log as a base. For building materials they use sticks and mud, perhaps adding a few stones. A mound is created. Most authorities say it is built in a hollow circle and then roofed over. But some lodges are built solid, the room inside being cut out afterward. At the peak of the cone-shaped structure, there is an opening for ventilation. There are usually two underwater entrances.

The room inside may be about six feet in diameter and two feet high. It is sometimes much larger. A six-foot man was able to stand upright in one large beaver lodge.

The floor is above water level. On it are beds made of shredded bark, which may be eaten if necessary.

Do beavers always live in lodges?

No. Some live in burrows dug out of the side of a bank. These burrows have an entrance, usually protected by tree roots, which is located just below the water line. The living chamber is above the water line. Air enters the burrow through a thin spot in the roof. Beavers that live in lodges often have a bank burrow or two as a refuge in which to hide when danger is present.

What kind of family life do beavers have?

In general, they lead a peaceful, close-knit family life. During the winter, the mother, the father, and their last two litters of young live together in the lodge. In the spring, the young beavers that are two years old leave home to establish their own families. The father also leaves at this time, but he will return when the new offspring are a couple of weeks old. The mother gives birth to two to six young.

Beavers mate for as long as they are both alive. The father works hard at keeping the lodge repaired and the food supply adequate.

At what time of day are you most likely to see a beaver?

Your best chance of getting a good look at a beaver in the wild is at dusk. Most beaver activity takes place at night. However, in areas where they are well protected, such as in our national parks, beavers may be out and around in the daytime.

White-Footed Mouse

*How do white-footed mice send
messages to one another?*

They tap with their feet on a smooth, hard surface, a
hollow reed, or a dry leaf. One theory is that they an-
nounce territorial possession with this drumming sound.
They also sing with a trilling or buzzing sound that can
be heard for quite a long way. Occasionally, they are
heard to give a clear, birdlike whistle.

Do white-footed mice climb trees?

Yes. They spend a good deal of time in trees. Their tails
aid them in maintaining balance if a twig starts to bend
beneath them.

What are other names for the white-footed mouse?

"Deer mouse" is probably the most common. The color-
ing of this dainty mouse resembles that of a deer, hence

the name. It is also called "wood mouse," since it often lives in the woods. "Vesper mouse" is still another name for it, because it comes out in the evening and sings.

By whatever name it is called, this big-eyed, big-eared, neat little mouse with the white "gloves" is a charmer. It is not only attractive but very fastidious about keeping its fur clean and well groomed. It should not be confused with its drab, untidy cousin, the house mouse.

How common are white-footed mice?

They are the most widespread of all North American rodents. They can adapt to almost any condition. Scarcely a square mile in the United States is without a white-footed mouse.

When are white-footed mice active?

They are active at night. White-footed mice see well in the darkness; in the sunlight, they act somewhat blinded.

Since they do not hibernate, mice have to worry about food all year. They store some seeds and nuts in the fall, but usually not enough to tide them over, so they have to leave their cozy winter homes in search of food. If there is snow on the ground, they tunnel beneath it.

Where do white-footed mice nest?

Sometimes they claim an abandoned squirrel or bird nest. At other times, they build a nest in a hollow log, under a rock or an old stump, or in a stone wall. They may take advantage of a burrow dug by another creature, or they may dig their own. Cracks and crevices in limestone cliffs may form the foundation for a nest. An empty cabin, an attic, or a basement may offer a temptation too great to be resisted.

The mother and father both work on remodeling an old nest or creating a new one. Soft materials such as grass, shredded bark, and cloth are used. The nest is globe-shaped and has the entrance on the side, near the top. This entrance has a plug, or "door," which can be closed for warmth.

What do white-footed mice eat?

Mostly seeds, grains, nuts, berries, small fruits, and insects. They do a certain amount of damage by eating tree bark and tree seeds, and by raiding grain fields or store-houses. They are less destructive, however, than the meadow mouse or the house mouse.

How long do they live?

It is possible for them to live eight years. Their life expectancy in the wild is three or four years, or perhaps less.

What animals eat mice?

All of the meat-eaters, even large creatures such as the bear and the cougar, eat mice. So do owls and hawks. Since they provide food for so many other animals, mice need to reproduce rapidly in order to survive.

*How many young does a white-footed
mouse have in a year?*

It is not at all uncommon for a female white-footed mouse to bear twenty-four young in a year. She has three to four litters a year, with an average of three to six young in each litter. She cares for them for about five weeks, and then they're on their own.

Why does the white-footed mouse keep changing its nest?

Although the mother is very careful to keep her own appearance neat, she is a sloppy housekeeper. She even uses the nest as a toilet. As a result, the nest soon becomes too fouled for raising a new litter. When she is about to give birth again, the mother leaves her family in the nest and builds a new one.

Muskrat

In an area where there might be muskrats,
what should you look for?

Muskrat houses are the most conspicuous evidence of
their presence. Although muskrats are active primarily at
night, you may see one sunning itself on a log or on its
house, or you may spot one eating grass along the bank
of a stream or swimming. When it is swimming, you will
first notice a V-shaped ripple; usually only the head of the
muskrat will be visible.

Other muskrat signs to look for are trails they have
made in the swamp, and piles or floating fragments of cattails or reeds.

Because muskrats are quiet animals, most active at night, many people think they are hard to spot. But my husband and I have seen them often in slow-moving water, especially on cloudy days. Even the noise of the motor on our boat does not scare them, unless we circle for a closer look. Then they are apt to dive underwater.

Where do muskrats live?

They build their houses in marshes, ponds, lakes, and slow-running streams. In fact, they can be found almost anyplace where there is water and where rushes, reeds, or cattails are available. Sometimes they build a cone-shaped lodge; sometimes they burrow into the bank for their home.

What kind of reputation do muskrats have as fighters?

They are very brave, even foolhardy at times. When cornered, they will fight to the last breath. They dash at the enemy, sometimes making a hissing noise as they do so.

They appear to be more aggressive on land than in the water. This is probably because they are not fast enough to escape by running. There have been reports of muskrats boldly defying a man when they are on land.

How does a muskrat get oxygen
when he is swimming under ice?

After a lake or a stream freezes, the water level will often go down. This creates a layer of air, or air pocket, underneath the ice. The muskrat comes to the surface to breathe this air. He can swim fifteen minutes before he needs to take another breath.

Some observers say that muskrats and beavers, if unable to find any air pocket under ice, will exhale, swim up, and rebreathe the air. Actually, animals (including man) do not use up all of the oxygen in a breath of air. It is this fact that makes mouth-to-mouth resuscitation possible.

How do the activities of the
muskrat and beaver compare?

Although the muskrat is closer to a meadow mouse than to any other creature, it has been called the "beaver's little brother." Like the beaver, it builds a cone-shaped lodge and uses burrows dug into the side of a bank. Muskrats, as well as beavers, dig tunnels. But muskrats do not chop down trees or build dams.

Muskrats build something beavers don't, however— eating huts. These are like their homes, except that they are smaller. Inside is a small feeding platform where the muskrat can dine without worrying about enemies or the weather. Muskrats also build feeding rafts. These are floating tangles of vegetation that are anchored to the bottom of the pond with a few stalks. They are convenient places to come out of the water and eat. When the pond freezes, the floating vegetation serves as a breathing hole for the muskrat. It is easy to keep an air hole open in the middle of the vegetation.

How do muskrat houses and beaver lodges compare?

Beaver lodges are usually much larger. The living chamber inside a muskrat house may be only about a foot in

diameter. The chamber of a beaver lodge may be large enough to hold a man. (In pioneer days, a white man once escaped hostile Indians by hiding in a beaver lodge.) However, muskrats add on to their houses in preparation for winter; as a result, the house sometimes becomes very large. Muskrat houses four feet above the water level and eight to ten feet in diameter are not uncommon.

Muskrat houses are not nearly so substantial as beaver houses, since they are made of cattails or reeds instead of sticks. Mud is the "cement" that holds both muskrat and beaver houses together. Both have underwater entrances, and both are kept exceedingly clean.

How do muskrats fix the roofs of their houses
when they begin to sag?

Outside, they add more material on top of the roof. Inside, they chew away at the ceiling to make it higher. Since the whole house is made of materials the muskrat considers edible, the house provides emergency food during severe winter weather.

What do muskrats eat?

A muskrat's diet consists mostly of vegetables. He pulls up water lilies, arrowheads, cattails, pondweeds, blue flags, wild rice, and bulrushes, and eats them, roots and all. From fields near the water, he gathers not only various weeds but also cultivated crops such as corn and alfalfa. If food is scarce, he eats bark. If he can catch them, he will eat such creatures as fish, crayfish, frogs, young birds, and small turtles. Clams appear to be a special favorite.

How long does a muskrat family stay together?

A very short period. The male muskrat does not help at all in caring for the young, and the mother is not especially conscientious in her maternal duties. The young are weaned by the time they are a month old, at which time the mother chases them from the lodge.

What are the main dangers a muskrat faces?

Outside of man, his biggest danger is a set of weather conditions that forces him out of his home, or seals him in it. A dry autumn followed by a severe winter may cause ice to freeze to the bottom of the ponds where muskrats live. Then they must decide whether to remain in their tomblike homes, which possibly means starvation, or to flee to land, where they are much more apt to fall victim to their natural enemies—hawks, owls, weasels, foxes, and coyotes.

In the water, young muskrats may become prey not only to mink, but also to snapping turtles and various fish such as pike and pickerel.

Are muskrats in danger of becoming extinct?

No, although they are extensively trapped. They have a life potential of about seven years, but most muskrats live only three or four years. Offsetting this is their rapid breeding rate. There are usually four to eight young in a litter. There may be as many as four litters in a year.

Porcupine

Are a "porcupine" and a "hedgehog" the same?

The porcupine is sometimes called a hedgehog, but it should not be. The quills of the North American porcupine and the Old World hedgehog are similar, and this is no doubt why the term hedgehog is sometimes used when porcupine is meant. The two animals are quite different. The porcupine is a rodent; the hedgehog is an insectivore.

Does a porcupine shoot its quills?

No. A porcupine occasionally can throw a few loosely attached quills about five feet by a flip of the tail. But strictly speaking, he does not shoot them. There are no quills on the face, the belly, or the underside of the tail. When attacked, a porcupine protects his face by lowering it between its front legs or hiding it under a nearby root or log. He arches his back and sticks his body quills out in every direction. He then turns his back to the enemy, for his tail is his offensive weapon. If the enemy attacks, the porcupine flips his tail up, down, and sideways. A bite by the attacker will result in a large number of quills being driven into the flesh around the mouth. The defense is extremely effective.

Why are a porcupine's quills so dangerous?

There are many barbs on each quill. As the quill enters the flesh, the barbs expand. With each movement of the victim, the quills work their way in deeper. They cannot be removed without tearing the flesh. Wild animals are unable to remove the quills and often die from them. Even humans need a pair of pliers and a strong pull to remove the quills.

When the porcupine is not afraid, can you see his quills?

The quills are controlled by a layer of muscle and can be made to lie flat or stick straight up. When a porcupine is relaxed, the quills on his body are hard to see because they are hidden in his fur, especially when the fur is thick, as it is in winter. Only on his tail can they be easily seen.

How many quills does a porcupine have?

About 30,000. When he is attacked, he discharges some of them, but he grows new ones to take their places. The quills are periodically shed and replaced, as is the fur.

What enemies does the porcupine have?

Because the porcupine kills a number of trees and can be a nuisance, man is his most deadly foe. But in the United States, man has also come close to killing off the porcupine's other most feared enemy—the fisher. Fishers have learned how to turn a porcupine over so they can attack its most vulnerable spot—its underbelly. Bobcats, lynxes, mountain lions, wolverines, and red foxes sometimes succeed in killing porcupines. Great horned owls that are desperate from hunger have been known to attack them.

Does the porcupine make any vocal sounds?

Porcupines make quite a few sounds, including a teeth-chattering which is regarded by some as being their main method of communication. They also grunt, squeak, growl, snarl, moan, cry like a child, whine, and sometimes bark or shriek. They sniff so loudly when searching for food or investigating danger that they can be heard several feet away. A meowing sound, which is sometimes called a song, is used during the mating season.

Can a porcupine swim?

Yes. A porcupine's quills are filled with air, and they hold the porcupine up when he is in the water. He does not swim well, but by paddling dog fashion he gets where he wants to go.

What do porcupines eat?

In winter, porcupines, which do not hibernate, eat the inner bark of various trees and the needles of evergreens. They are particularly fond of hemlock, white pine, and yellow pine. When spring comes, they eat the catkins and blossoms of certain trees, and tender young leaves. In summer, they vary their diet with plants, nuts, and fruit. Water lilies, arrowhead leaves, and corn seem to be especially desired.

Porcupines have a great craving for salt and will eat anything with even a faint flavor of salt. This includes such things as the handles of farm tools, axes, and hammers; saddles; and canoe paddles. They are also very fond of bones, which provide them with minerals.

What kind of den do porcupines have?

They choose a hollow log or stump, a cave, a hole under tree roots, a brushpile, or a spot under a rock ledge. An old deserted building may become home for a number of porcupines. In winter, they spend much of their time in trees.

Does the father take part in caring for the young?

No. Usually, only one porcupine is born at a time, although there may occasionally be twins. The young porcupine nurses from his mother for several weeks. The young are sometimes playful. Even adult porcupines have been seen standing on their hind legs, rocking to and fro and waving their paws in rhythmic exercise. However, there does not seem to be much display of affection between the mother porcupine and her young one. The youngster sticks around for about six months and then wanders off for increasingly long periods until all contact is lost.

Is a porcupine stupid?

Old-timers often call porcupines "the stupidest things in the woods." This belief was based on many incidents. Even when shot at, porcupines would keep on returning to camp. A porcupine once ate a third of a stick of dynamite. Another porcupine walked up to a man who was standing very still and started to eat the leather puttees he was wearing on his legs.

However, experiments in the laboratory have revealed that the porcupine is not all that stupid. Poor eyesight and a strong sense of curiosity combine to give him an undeserved reputation. The reason so many porcupines are killed on the highway is because they are unable to move fast.

Wolf

Is the eastern timber wolf the same as the gray wolf?

It is one kind of gray wolf. The eastern timber wolf is the only kind of wolf found in significant numbers in the forty-eight contiguous states. It is the one most of us think of in response to the word "wolf."

Other wolves found in the United States are the red wolf and the northern Rocky Mountain wolf, both of which are rare. The red wolf is found in Texas and Louisi-

ana. No one knows how many are left—estimates range from one hundred to three hundred. The name of the northern Rocky Mountain wolf gives you an idea of where it is found. Not long ago this wolf was believed to be extinct, but it is now known that there are about twenty left in the United States. Mexican wolves are occasionally seen in southern United States, but it is likely that most of these wolves have traveled south across the Mexican border.

How can you tell wolves, coyotes, and foxes apart?

Size is the main factor. The timber wolf is about twice as big as the coyote, and the coyote, in turn, is much bigger than the fox. In size and appearance, a timber wolf looks like an exceptionally large gray German shepherd dog; the coyote like a grayish, medium-sized dog; the fox like a small dog.

The tails are also helpful in distinguishing these animals. The coyote is the only one that holds its tail down when it runs. Wolves and foxes hold theirs high. The red fox, our most common fox, has a very bushy, white-tipped tail.

You can tell a wolf from a German shepherd dog because the wolf's legs are noticeably longer.

Will wolves attack a man?

The U.S. Fish and Wildlife Service conducted a twenty-five-year study of cases where wolves had supposedly made unprovoked attacks on men in North America. None of these stories could be proved. Since then, a case occurred in which a railroad worker in Ontario was attacked by a wolf. Unfortunately, the wolf could not be caught and tested for rabies; however, the behavior of this particular wolf has led Dr. L. David Mech and other experts on wolves to believe that the animal was rabid.

Wolves are curious, and they might well surround a man without intending to attack him. However, a man surrounded by wolves would probably expect an attack and would be inclined to credit his "escape" to his own cleverness or good fortune.

Dr. Adolph Murie once entered a wolf den that contained pups. The parents moved some distance away and howled and barked at him, but they did nothing to prevent him from taking one of the pups with him. This is hardly the way a man-eating beast would react. Another indication of the wolf's relatively passive nature is the fact that researchers are able to handle wild wolves without using drugs.

It is now generally believed that "man-eating wolves" were rabid animals, and that a healthy wolf will not attack a man.

What is a wolf pack?

A pack is usually a family unit. It most often consists

of parents and their young. Young wolves may stay with their parents until they are two or three years old. A pack may contain from two to twenty wolves, but the average number is six.

Why is it important for wolves to be in a pack?

Wolves often feed on large animals such as the moose, the weight of which can equal that of twelve wolves. It takes the cooperation of several wolves to make such a kill. Even the pack often fails. The group structure of the pack makes it easier to provide food for members who cannot "carry their own weight"—the pups and the aged.

What is wolf family life like?

Wolves are affectionate and loyal, both as mates and as parents. Most authorities believe that wolves mate for life. The father shares in the care of the young. The mother gives birth in a den that is located in a cave, a large crack in the rocks, a hole dug by the mother, or one dug by a smaller animal and enlarged by the mother.

During the first two weeks, the mother stays in the den with the young, and the other members of the pack bring food to her. After that, the father and some other members of the pack are allowed in the den. All members of the pack help with the young, feeding them, playing with them, caring for them while the mother hunts. When the young are six to eight weeks old, they begin to travel short distances with the pack. Soon afterward, they leave the den and sleep outdoors with the others.

While the young are in the den, the father guards it when he is not hunting. In case of danger, he tries to lure the enemy away from the den. If anything happens to the mother, he takes over the care of the young.

What sounds do wolves make?

Most of the sounds are similar to those of a domestic

dog. Parents use a soft whine or a whimper when calling their pups. There are howls that seem to be used to call together other members of the pack, and howls that simply express emotion. There are barks of alarm and challenge, and squeals when pups are too rough in their play. Wolves pursuing an animal give short barking sounds like a pack of hounds. They snarl when killing prey.

The sounds a wolf makes are sometimes ventriloquial, which makes it difficult at times to tell how many wolves are howling or from what direction the howls are coming.

What do wolves eat?

Their big game includes moose, deer, elk, pronghorns, bighorn sheep, and caribou. When they are near civilization, they may kill livestock. Small animals in their diet include pocket gophers, rabbits, ground squirrels, mice, and beavers. Wolves sometimes eat berries and vegetable matter.

What effect does the wolf have on other wildlife?

Most of the kills wolves make are of excess young, or of animals that are ill, wounded, or aged. The net result is that wolves keep a herd of prey animals in top condition. They also tend to keep the population of the prey animals steady.

Isle Royale National Park provides an excellent spot for studying the populations of wolves and moose, because of its isolated location and the fact that no hunting is allowed. Although the wolves prey on the moose, the moose are, if anything, actually increasing in number.

How do wolves decide whether or not to attack a moose?

They test it by surrounding it and making cautious leaps in its direction. If the moose does not run but stands its ground, the wolves generally give up the effort after a few minutes.

*Under what conditions is it easy
for wolves to kill a deer?*

When there is a great deal of snow, deer often gather together in deer "yards." It is much easier for wolves to kill them here. Ordinarily, when a deer is startled by wolves, the deer has a good chance of outrunning them. With its long legs, it can jump over fallen logs, boulders and thick brush. The wolf, with its much shorter legs, is at a disadvantage.

Is the wolf an endangered animal in the United States?

Yes. The eastern timber wolf, the red wolf, and the northern Rocky Mountain wolf are all on the endangered species list. All are protected by federal law in the forty-eight contiguous states. A decrease in wilderness areas where the wolf can exist and relentless persecution by man have made this intelligent and interesting animal almost extinct. Man is the wolf's only enemy.

In the United States today, timber wolves are found in significant numbers only in northern Minnesota and in Alaska. From 1969 through 1973, Minnesota had a pred-ator-control program under which registered trappers were allowed to trap wolves that were doing damage to livestock or wildlife. Minnesota officials believe that this program is better than one of complete protection for the wolf. As a result of the success of the program, Minnesota is currently asking federal officials to remove the wolf from the endangered species list in that state.

In Alaska, wolves are controlled by state regulation rather than by federal law. Hunting wolves from aircraft was once a common practice in Alaska, but this practice is now illegal. Alaska no longer pays bounties for wolves.

Coyote

Why do coyotes howl?

The howl of the coyote is a social gesture. Just as two people may sit and talk with each other at dusk, a pair of coyotes raise their voices in a duet of howling. The song is often picked up by other coyotes, distant but within hearing range. "We are all here, and all is well," is probably the most common message conveyed by the give-and-take of these howls. Howling may also indicate loneliness, tell of danger, or be a call for assistance.

To people who love animals, the howl of the coyote is usually regarded as a thrilling sound. It has become a symbol of the western prairie.

What are other common names for the coyote?

"Brush wolf" and "prairie wolf" are two of the most common. They are both appropriate, because the coyote is a creature of the open plains or brushland, in contrast to the timber wolf, which prefers forests. "Steppenwolf" is another name for the coyote.

Why do coyotes confine most of their activities to the nighttime?

Primarily because bitter experience has taught them they are apt to be shot if they are seen by man in the daytime. Coyotes used to hunt in the daytime, especially early in the morning and at dusk. Now they only do so in areas that are wild enough that very few humans are around.

Do coyotes have a close-knit family life?

Yes. Coyotes usually stick to one mate for several years, and sometimes for life. The father is very conscientious. He cares for his mate when she is pregnant or nursing by bringing her food. When the young ones arrive, he helps to feed and protect them. When danger threatens, he tries to lure the enemy away from the spot where his family is hidden. If anything happens to the mother, he takes over care of the young, provided they are old enough to eat meat. Both parents train the young in the art of hunting. The young ones stay with their parents until fall, or sometimes through the first winter.

What kind of den do coyotes have?

Coyote dens may be located almost anywhere—in a rocky cave, a drainage pipe, a burrow that has been abandoned or that they have dug themselves. They prefer the side of a hill, not too far from water. They do not usually bother with any nesting material, but they do keep the den very clean and free of litter. There is often a hole in the ceiling for ventilation.

Coyotes don't live in a den the year round. When the young are old enough, the family leaves, seeking shelter wherever it is convenient. But the parents will probably return to the same den the following year to raise their young.

Why does the female coyote prepare several dens?

Coyotes often move the young from one den to another. They do this whenever humans come close enough to the den that the coyotes fear for their young. Sometimes, the move is necessary to get away from an excess of fleas. Females have been known to prepare as many as twelve dens before the pups are born.

Do coyotes cooperate in hunting?

Yes. Although coyotes sometimes hunt alone, they often hunt in pairs or family groups. Cooperation is necessary when they are attacking a large animal such as a deer. Even in twos and threes, they seldom attack an animal this size unless the animal is sick or wounded.

Coyotes have a well-organized system of running down smaller prey such as jack rabbits. One coyote rests while the other chases. As the rabbit begins to circle, the second coyote cuts across the center of the circle and takes up the chase. Now the first coyote rests. This relay chase is continued until the rabbit is exhausted. Then he is easy to catch.

Oddly enough, a coyote and a badger will sometimes hunt together. The badger digs out a small animal, perhaps a gopher. If the gopher escapes the badger, the coyote gets it. If the coyote chases a small animal into a hole, the badger digs it out and has himself a meal.

What proof is there that a
coyote is a clever animal?

In spite of relentless persecution by man, the coyote has managed to extend its range. It is now found almost everywhere in North America except in parts of eastern United States.

Coyotes are extremely adaptable. They take advantage of all kinds of situations in which their potential food may be flushed out. They have been seen following cattle, bulldozers, and snowplows; when mice or rodents scurried out of the way of these "monsters," the coyote was on hand to grab a meal.

Does the coyote have enemies
other than man?

Pups and sometimes adults may be killed by bears, wolves, cougars, and golden eagles. Adults are sometimes killed by deer or elk. But the coyote's only important enemy is man.

Do coyotes kill large numbers of sheep?

Woolgrowers say "yes"; many conservationists say "no." Coyotes probably do man more good than harm. Their habits of eating rabbits, rodents, mice, insects, and dead animals are beneficial to man. As a rule, livestock are only a very small part of the coyote's diet. One western state that practically exterminated coyotes found, in a few years, that it had a very serious problem with ground squirrels. Some ranchers now protect coyotes on their land, because otherwise they lose too much of their hay crop to small animals on which the coyote feeds.

A sheep-killing coyote is apt to be one that is old or crippled from having been caught in a trap. Such animals kill fewer rodents and rabbits because they are unable to catch them.

Scientists have now proposed a method of satisfying both sheep ranchers and conservationists. By taking the flesh of a lamb and treating it so that severe illness follows eating it, they have produced a bait that cures the coyote of sheep killing. Tests have been very successful; coyotes who have eaten the treated flesh once or twice would have nothing whatsoever to do with a live lamb when given the chance. Surely this technique is preferable to the slaughtering of coyotes by poison or trapping.

Red Fox

Is the red fox as crafty as he is reputed to be?

Yes, both as the hunted and as the hunter. He makes his trail difficult to follow by entering water, running along the top of a stone wall or fence, or doubling back in his own footsteps. As an example of his cleverness in hunting, he will play with a stick on shore to arouse the curiosity of ducks in the water. Then he stops playing and hides, and a duck or two may wander on shore to see what was going on. When this happens, the fox leaps out from his hiding place.

America's
Best Loved
Wild Animals

How fast can a fox move?

Ordinarily, when he is trotting along in search of something to eat, a fox goes about five miles an hour. But some foxes can gallop at forty-five miles an hour. People in cars have clocked them at this speed more than once. However, they cannot maintain this rate for more than a mile or so, and the normal maximum speed is about twenty-eight miles an hour.

Why is the fox regarded as a playful animal?

The pups have mock battles, games of tag and hide-and-seek, as the young of most animals do. But the adults like to play as well, which is not so common. They will make a game out of playing with a stick or a stone, as a dog will do. Foxes have even been known to play with domestic dogs and to try to play with such animals as bighorn sheep, cattle, and elk. The fox leaps about, rubbing against the other animal and gently nibbling at its face. Sometimes a game of tag develops.

Do foxes have territories?

Yes. A fox spends most of the time between sunset and sunrise traveling about his territory. Some of this traveling is for the purpose of hunting food, but some is for patroling the territory. In addition to foxes who have settled territories, there are always others who are on the move, seeking a place to live. When a fox family is killed, the location is taken over by other foxes.

Under certain circumstances, when there is a great abundance of food, foxes do not seem to mind if another fox family moves into the territory. Then two families may share one den.

Does the father help care for the young foxes?

Usually he does. Apparently some fathers pay little attention to their young. But the majority bring food to both mother and pups during the period when the young are nursing. Then, when the pups are older, both parents work at bringing food home to the young. Red fox parents frequently display a great deal of affection for their offspring and for each other. It is believed they sometimes mate for life.

Do foxes live in a den all year?

No. The den serves as a nursery, but as soon as the pups are old enough, the family leaves it. During the rest of the year, they sleep aboveground, seeking shelter in tangles of brush, rocky hideouts, long grass, hedges, or overgrown ditches.

Foxes like dens in sandy or loamy soil. They prefer open land, such as a pasture, fence border, or cultivated field. They usually choose a hilltop or slope where they can keep a good lookout and where the water will drain away. They like the den to face south or east. Often they enlarge holes dug by badgers or woodchucks. There may be a number of entrances.

If the den is molested or if there are too many parasites, the parents pick up the pups in their mouths and carry them to another den.

How long do fox pups stay with their parents?

The pups begin to come out of the den when they are about one month old. At first, they peek out and hurry back in. Before long, they begin to play together near the den. I once watched some fox pups playing in front of their den. Their mother was trotting away from the den when I first saw her. She soon became aware that there were humans nearby. She paused, started back toward the den, and barked. The young ones hurried inside the den. Then the mother trotted off over the hill, either to resume her hunting or to lure us away from the den.

About the time the young are four months old, they

leave the den and follow their parents. By the end of summer, most of the youngsters have wandered off on their own.

How can you recognize a fox den?

In late winter, foxes clean out old dens for use as a nursery. There is often snow on the ground at this time, and so the dirt around the den entrance shows plainly. As the pups grow up and the parents feed them outside the den, the area becomes littered with the remains of the animals eaten. There is a strong "foxy" odor about the place.

How do foxes communicate with one another?

Many of the sounds they make are similar to those of a dog. They bark, snarl, growl, howl, whimper, and whine. They sometimes let out a bloodcurdling shriek. Mothers use murmuring sounds to call their cubs and a coughing bark to warn them of danger.

Foxes also communicate with one another by scent. There are scent glands located on the bottoms of their feet. By scent-marking a trail, foxes can keep track of one another. The urine is used as a scent signal as well.

What do foxes eat?

Their principal foods are rabbits and mice. They also eat other small mammals, although they don't seem to care much for moles, shrews, and weasels. They apparently dislike the musky odor. Foxes eat a wide range of foods, including ground-nesting birds, earthworms, insects, berries, fruits, vegetables, dead animals, and garbage.

They have been accused of reducing the number of game birds and of killing poultry. However, the fox population does not seem to have much effect on the number of game birds in an area. Efficient methods of raising poultry can keep the chickens safe from foxes.

Do foxes store food?

Yes. When they have more food than they can eat, they dig a hole to hide it, then cover it with leaves, dirt, or snow. Later, they may dig it up, just to be sure it is there, then re-cover it. These are just temporary food stores, however. They don't store up food for the winter as a chipmunk does.

Why does the fox have so few enemies?

Most of the predators that might enjoy a meal of fox are unable to catch him. Great horned owls and eagles may take a fox pup now and then. Wolves, coyotes, lynxes, bobcats, mountain lions, and wolverines can occasionally catch and kill an adult fox as well as a pup. Men, hunting dogs, and various diseases are the fox's worst enemies.

Black Bear

Are black bears always black?

No. They are often brown. A mother may give birth to black cubs one year and brown the next. There may be a brown cub and a black cub in the same litter.

The blue, or glacier, bear of Alaska and the white Kermode's bear found in British Columbia are also classified as black bears.

Are bears true hibernators?

No. The body temperature of a bear does not drop much during its winter sleep. Its breathing rate remains nearly normal. Consequently, the winter sleep of a bear is not regarded as true hibernation.

How deep the bear's sleep is seems to depend somewhat on the individual bear and how fat it was when it entered the winter sleep. One scientist who has studied bears illustrates the difference by two experiences he has had. In one case, a bear came snorting out of its winter den as he approached. In the other case, he broke through the snow covering of a den and landed right on top of the sleeping bear! In this case, fortunately, the bear was sleeping very soundly and did not even awaken when a large man landed on top of her.

It is not unusual for a bear to come out of its winter den for a few hours or days when the weather is mild.

What kind of den does the bear like?

Bears prefer to den under an uprooted tree, in a large hollow tree, or in a cave. If they cannot find such a spot, they will dig themselves a den or settle for a dense thicket.

The young are born in the den during the winter sleep of the mother. There are usually two of them, each smaller than a newborn porcupine. The father sleeps in a separate den and takes no part in care of the young.

What does the black bear do with
her cubs if danger threatens?

She sends them up a tree. She makes them obey her by giving them a cuff with her paw on their rumps. If necessary, she may insist that they stay up in the tree for hours. She also sends them up a tree if she wants to leave them for a while. When it is time for them to come down, she lets them know by calling to them with a whimpering sound.

Are bears playful?

Yes. Not only bear cubs, but adults as well, like to slide down slippery slopes on their rumps. Sometimes a bear will rock back and forth on his haunches or turn a somer-

sault. Mates wrestle and box playfully or stand upright and hug each other. Bears have even been known to play with another kind of animal, such as a coyote.

What do bears eat?

Almost anything. In the spring they eat roots of such plants as the crocus and the wild onion. They like fruit, berries, nuts, clover, corn, and the buds and leaves of certain trees. Their well-known love of honey reveals their sweet tooth. They are meat eaters as well. Their tastes include insects, mice, birds, marmots, chipmunks, ground squirrels, frogs, trout, and salmon.

Occasionally a bear will acquire the habit of killing

domestic animals such as sheep and goats, and must be destroyed. In the national parks, bears have developed a fondness for garbage and handouts.

Can bears climb?

Yes. All bears, including polar bears, are able to climb. Black bears are expert climbers. Their paws are rough on the surface, inward curving, and equipped with long claws —all adaptations for climbing. Black bears often rest or sleep in trees. Grizzlies are able to climb but, because of their weight, are not apt to do so.

Can bears swim?

Yes. They are good swimmers. They can swim for several miles, and if they are near water when they are wounded, they may try to save themselves by entering the water.

What kind of tracks do bears leave?

Bear tracks look a great deal like those of a barefooted human.

What is a "bear tree"?

It is a tree that has been marked by the claws and teeth of a bear. When he is about to mark such a tree, a bear will stand up on his hind legs, embrace the tree trunk with his paws, and then bite and claw the tree until he has satisfied his urge.

Bear trees are always located on well-worn paths and are used by many different bears. One explanation of this activity is that these marks serve as signposts. For example, if a small bear comes ambling along the trail and sees that a much larger bear has recently left his mark, he may decide to change his direction. Another explanation is that the bears use these trees to stretch their muscles and relax.

What enemies does the black bear have?

Man is the principal enemy. Grizzly bears and cougars sometimes kill black bears. Wolves may attack the cubs, or an adult sleeping in a poorly protected winter den. Black bears have died as a result of attacking porcupines. A mouth full of quills may leave a bear unable to eat, causing him to die of starvation.

*What should you do if you meet
a black bear in the wild?*

First of all, if you're going anyplace where there might be a bear, you should make quite a bit of noise. This gives the bear the opportunity to hear you and get out of your way. Unless they are half-tame, bears are very shy. If you do meet a black bear, experienced naturalists usually advise standing still and shouting. A number of people have used this strategy successfully.

Feeding of bears in our national parks is forbidden, because such handouts encourage these half-tame bears to beg for food and then to rob. Some of these bears become aggressive to the point where they will injure or even kill a human.

Raccoon

How can you recognize a raccoon?

The raccoon is a medium-sized, grayish animal that is very easy to recognize by the black mask across his pointed face and the black rings on his bushy tail.

You can often tell if there are raccoons about by their footprints in the mud or dust. The print of their front paws resembles that of a small human hand.

Why is the raccoon regarded
as being very courageous?

The raccoon would rather flee than fight, and it uses many of the same tricks a fox uses to lose its pursuers. But when cornered, it is a ferocious fighter. It is said that a healthy, full-grown raccoon can always beat a dog of the same size and weight. It has been known to defend itself successfully against two or three dogs, each much larger than itself.

Because it is such an expert at self-defense, the raccoon has few enemies except man and his dogs.

Is it true that raccoons always wash
their food before eating it?

No. If there is no water handy, a raccoon will eat his food anyway. The latest research indicates that it is primarily *captive* raccoons that insist on dipping their food into water before eating it.

Water increases the sensitivity of a raccoon's hands. As a result, raccoons can feel their food better in water. It is probably this fact or an expression of playfulness, rather than a desire to wash their food, that causes raccoons to dunk what they eat.

What do raccoons eat?

As a general rule, raccoons eat more vegetables and fruits than meat. Corn and crayfish are favorite delicacies, but they won't turn down a chance to dine on frogs, snails, or mussels. Berries, melons, and nuts are eaten when available. They like fish, which they can sometimes catch in shallow water. Turtle eggs, bird eggs, insects, earthworms, grubs, and mice provide an added source of food. Raccoons occasionally steal chickens, but this does not happen often.

Where do raccoons live?

Raccoons like hollow trees. You can sometimes coax them into sticking their heads out of an entrance hole in a hollow tree by giving the tree a hard rap, since they are very curious. They prefer to nest in a hollow that is high in a tree and gets plenty of sun. If this isn't available, they will nest in a hollow nearer the ground, or even on the ground. Sometimes they must settle for a crevice in a rocky ledge, an abandoned burrow, or a small cave. They have also been known to den in such places as machine sheds, haylofts, or piles of lumber.

They are most apt to be found near water, since many of their favorite foods are found in or near the water.

What kind of family life do raccoons have?

The young, usually four or five of them, are born in April or May. In late June, the baby raccoons can sometimes be seen sunning themselves on a limb high in a tree. By July, they follow their mother in nighttime excursions for food. The mother shows great courage in protecting her young. If pursued by dogs, she sometimes takes the youngsters up a tree and then runs off, leading the dogs on a chase. Unless she is killed, she will return to her young when the danger is past.

The young remain with the mother until the next spring. Sometimes the father spends the winter in the same den with them.

Are raccoons sociable?

Yes. Several of them are often found together in a tree den, and they frequently hunt together in family groups of three to six.

Do raccoons hibernate?

They go into a winter sleep, but it is not true hibernation. Their body temperature remains the same throughout the winter. They wake up in warm spells and go searching for mice or rabbits to eat.

Raccoons put on much extra weight in the fall, but they do not store food. When they come out in the spring, food is very scarce. They live off their body fat until food is available. They are sometimes pathetically thin by the time this occurs.

What sounds does a raccoon make?

Young raccoons begging for food make a sound like a soft "orr-orr-orr." When hurt or hungry, they cry and whimper. Adult coons growl, snarl, and hiss when upset or angry, but their normal conversation is composed of a variety of churring sounds. When they are pleased, they actually purr. They also use a call, "whoo-oo-oo," a long-drawn-out, quivering song that resembles the call of a screech owl but is louder and harsher.

How do raccoons rate as pets?

If they have become pets at a young age, they are interesting, lovable, and affectionate. They are very intelligent and adaptable, but some of them become rather cranky with age.

The difficulty with having raccoons as pets is that they are extremely curious, mischievous, and skilled at doing things they shouldn't. They use their front paws much like human hands, picking up objects to examine them or to eat them. They can learn to turn doorknobs and can easily get into a cupboard or pantry. They then proceed to pry covers off jam jars and do all kinds of mischief. Life with a raccoon for a pet is rarely dull.

Mink

*Why is the mink considered less
destructive than the weasel?*

The mink is not noted for his good disposition, but he
is not so bloodthirsty as his close relative, the weasel.
When a weasel gets into a henhouse, he sometimes goes
on a rampage, killing much more than he can eat; on occasion, he will kill every single chicken.

A mink is more apt to take just one or two chickens at
a time. Once in a while, an individual mink will behave
like a weasel. He will kill half a dozen chickens and eat
only the parts he likes best—the blood and brains. But
this appears to be the exception.

How do mink get around?

They sometimes walk with a slow, lumbering gait. More often, they move by means of a series of leaps. They are excellent swimmers.

What does the mink have in common with the skunk?

When a mink gets irritated or excited, he discharges a liquid that has a smell much like that of a skunk. Most people think the mink's smell is worse than the skunk's. The mink cannot spray his musk as a skunk can, but he releases it more often.

Where does the mink live?

The den is usually located near a wooded stream or lake or in a marsh. A hollow log, a hole under tree roots, a crevice in a rock, or a burrow in a bank may provide shelter. The mink is fond of eating muskrat, and after devouring them he may take over the muskrat house.

Does the father help care for the young?

The male mates with several females during the breeding season. But he stays with the last one. He then settles down and helps care for the young. The family breaks up in late summer, each member going its own way.

How does a mink carry its young?

On land, the parents pick up the young by the scruffs of the necks. In the water, the young get a ride on the parents' backs.

What do mink eat?

As we have noted, mink enjoy muskrats and chickens. They also eat fish, snakes, frogs, crayfish, insects, rats, mice, rabbits, red squirrels, birds, and eggs. The mink is perfectly capable of catching his own fish, diving into the water after he has spotted a fish from his lookout on the bank of the stream. He has also been known to steal the catch of a human who has been fishing.

What enemies does the mink have?

The mink is fast and ferocious, and not many animals prey on him. The great horned owl is his worst enemy. The fox, the bobcat, the lynx, and the snowy owl occasionally are able to catch and kill mink.

Are mink becoming rare?

No. Although there are never great numbers of them in any one place, they can be found in most parts of the United States. Civilization does not seem to have affected them much. They even live in such large cities as New York—wherever conditions are right for them. Because they are usually out only at night, they may be nearby without people being aware of them.

How can you tell a mink from similar animals?

About the size of a small house cat, the mink is smaller than the otter or the fisher. Minks are chocolate brown in color, with a white patch on the chin. The weasel has white or yellowish underparts, and the marten has a buff-colored patch on the throat and breast.

The mink does not hibernate. Neither does it change into a white winter coat, as does its relative, the ermine.

Badger

Why can't you dig a badger out of its hole?

A badger can move through the soil faster than a man can dig with a shovel. If surprised above the ground, he can disappear into the ground in ninety seconds or so, digging furiously with all four feet, using his mouth as well. He can outdig a pocket gopher or a mole, and that takes a bit of doing!

What kind of behavior can you expect
from a badger if you meet one?

If the badger is close to one of his holes (and he has many), he will probably scurry down into it. He may go frontward or backward, whichever is handier. Or he may dig himself underground in a hurry.

If there isn't a hole handy, however, the badger may decide to fight. He apparently believes the best defense is a good offense. My husband and I once met a badger while we were walking down a country road that was overgrown with weeds. When he saw us, the badger turned about and began to shuffle on ahead of us in the narrow rut. He soon changed his mind, turned around, and began running toward us. Then it was our turn to change direction. After a bit, we stopped and looked around to see what was happening. At this, the badger turned, and began to move rapidly away from us. We started to follow him again. He stopped in his tracks, turned around, and came after us a second time. We decided not to tangle with him.

The actions of this badger were quite typical. Badgers are very bold. A mother badger with her young ones once defied an automobile until her offspring got across the road. Often the badger is bluffing and will retreat at the last minute, but you can't really depend on that. They are ferocious fighters. They fight a man by snapping at his legs.

*What advantage does a badger
have in a fight with a dog?*

The badger's skin is so loose and its hair so heavy that a dog cannot sink its teeth into a badger and injure it, as it can with other animals. A badger's teeth and claws are very sharp and its jaws are exceedingly strong, so it has good weapons for fighting back. A badger is capable of holding off a whole pack of dogs while it works its way to a hole into which it can disappear.

It is said that a badger's courage is so great that it never surrenders. Because it is so capable of taking care of itself, it has few natural enemies.

How can you recognize a badger?

A badger is a medium-sized, silvery-gray animal with black and white markings on its face. The narrow white stripe on the forehead runs partway down the back. A broad body that appears flattened and extremely short legs give the badger an awkward gait and the appearance of waddling along without legs. He is pigeon-toed, and his front claws are a couple of inches long.

Badgers live primarily on the plains and in the desert.

Are badgers playful?

They have their lighter moments. Badgers have been observed wrestling together and play-fighting, as dogs do. Captive badgers make up all sorts of games with a stick, a ball, or a dish. They will toss it into the air and catch it, stalk it, and pounce on it. They occasionally skip and dance about. Apparently British badgers, which differ considerably from American badgers, are even more playful.

If taken young, badgers make friendly, interesting pets.

What kind of family life does the badger have?

The young, usually two or three of them, are born in May or June. Their nest is a grass-lined room at the end of a long tunnel, and it is two to six feet underground. When the youngsters are about two-thirds grown, the mother takes them along with her on hunting expeditions. Occasionally the father sticks around to help take care of the young. The family separates in the fall.

What kinds of sounds does a badger make?

When he is engaged in a fight, a badger makes hissing noises, squeals, snarls, and growls. He grunts when fighting, but he also grunts to express pleasure.

What do badgers eat?

They are meat eaters. They dine principally on ground squirrels, gophers, and other underground dwellers. Mice, rabbits, ground-nesting birds and their eggs, snakes, and insects are also acceptable items for a badger.

Do badgers hibernate?

Strictly speaking, no, although in the extreme northern part of their range they sleep throughout the winter. In the south, they stay active all year. In most parts of their range, badgers plug their den entrances with dirt and sleep for two or three weeks at a time in winter. They come out of their dens when they get hungry. They may dig out a ground squirrel or a skunk from its winter den, or catch a cottontail aboveground. If there is more food than they can eat, they bury the remainder and dig it out later.

Why are badgers decreasing in number?

Badgers have been poisoned and trapped because they are nuisances. Their habit of digging many holes makes them disliked by cattlemen. Cattle and horses sometimes stumble in a badger hole and may break a leg. There is less land available now to badgers, since they move out, as a rule, when fields are cultivated. There are also fewer gophers and ground squirrels, the main sources of food for a badger.

Do badgers do man more harm than good?

No. They do more good than harm. Their burrows may be a nuisance, but they eat many crop-consuming rodents, poisonous snakes, and insects.

Skunk

Is it the skunk's urine that has such a foul odor?

No. The skunk has two special glands located under his tail which discharge the fluid musk that other animals find so very offensive. Apparently even skunks dislike the smell, for they avoid getting the spray on themselves and don't often use it in a fight with another skunk.

Will a skunk sometimes "hold his fire"
in the presence of humans?

Yes. If you don't startle the skunk by sudden movement or loud noises, he is not apt to pay much attention to you. My father once followed a few feet behind a skunk along a forest trail. The skunk was aware of my father's presence but ignored him, and finally turned off into the woods.

A dramatic illustration of a skunk's holding fire happened to a friend of mine. He came upon a skunk which had its head caught inside an empty tin can. The skunk was banging the can against the ground in futile attempts to free itself. Summoning all of his courage, my friend went to the rescue. Wearing gloves, talking softly and soothingly to the skunk, he removed the can from the skunk's head. The skunk, free, gave his head a shake, looked at my friend with what must have been gratitude, and took off into the woods.

What warnings does a skunk give
before spraying an enemy?

If you come upon a skunk in the outdoors, it will first express its displeasure, if it feels you are getting too close, by stamping its feet and growling. It may prepare for attack by facing you; more likely, it will turn its back. The next warning it gives is to raise and spread its tail, all but the very tip. The final warning the skunk gives is to raise the tip. If it is facing away from you, it will arch its back and lower its head so that it can see better, and then look around. Its aim is very good.

Ernest Thompson Seton, the famous naturalist, advises that, if you find yourself in line of fire from an angry skunk, your best hope of avoiding disaster is to stand perfectly still. It is all right to talk softly, but don't move. He may reconsider, lower his tail, and be on his way. But it is much safer to retreat at the very first warning signal.

If you do get sprayed, tomato juice, diluted ammonia, and turpentine have all been recommended for washing away the smell.

How far can a skunk throw his spray?

Up to about twelve feet, or farther if the wind is right. He can spray five or six times. If he has just used the spray, he may be low on "ammunition" or even out of it. It takes a while for the sacs to refill with fluid.

Skunks can aim their spray forward or backward with great accuracy.

Is there more than smell involved in
the skunk's method of defense?

Yes. The liquid that the skunk sprays on his victim is an irritating chemical. In the eyes, it may cause temporary blindness and will bring about a great flowing of tears. However, no permanent damage will be done to the eyes. It also causes intense smarting, burning, and sometimes swelling of the tissues lining the nose, throat, and mouth. It may cause faintness and violent nausea.

What is the everyday life of a skunk like?

He eats mostly insects, rodents—such as mice and ground squirrels—berries, and fruits. Wasps, beetles, and grasshoppers are the insects he devours most frequently. Game birds and eggs make up about one per cent of his diet.

Meal hunting is done at night, since the skunk usually rests or sleeps in the daytime. The skunk does not get out of the way for any other creature. Even bears have been observed to step off the trail for him. His only enemies, except for man, are the great horned owl, the barred owl, or a desperately hungry meat eater such as a fox or coyote.

Skunks don't hibernate, but they do sleep off and on throughout the winter.

What kind of family life do skunks have?

The female skunk finds herself a den. She may dig one in the side of a bank, make use of one abandoned by a badger or woodchuck, enlarge the chamber of a ground squirrel, or settle for shelter under an old building. The young are usually born in April or May. There may be only two or as many as ten. The male does not help care for the young.

By the middle of summer, the young ones begin to follow single file behind the mother in her nightly food-hunting expeditions. Some of the young males become independent and wander off by themselves in late summer. That winter, the remaining members of the family, sometimes including the father, curl up together for warmth in one den. In the spring, before the new family arrives, the old family scatters.

Do skunks ever make a noise?

They are usually quite silent. But they do growl, snarl, scream, or give a hoarse bark when angry, and make twittering, grunting, or chirping noises when they are happy. When they are investigating something that arouses their curiosity, they make a sniffing noise.

Can skunks climb trees?

Not the common striped skunk. It can climb a wire-mesh fence but seems unable to master climbing a tree. However, the spotted skunk, which has short stripes and spots and is much smaller, is a good climber.

What kind of disposition do skunks have?

They are usually mild and good-natured, although the males sometimes fight one another during the mating season. They have little to fear, so they move about slowly and calmly. Many are hit by automobiles as a result. They use their spray only as a last resort. With the scent glands removed, skunks make affectionate, easy-to-manage pets.

Are skunks becoming rare?

No. There may be more of them now than there were before the arrival of the white man in North America. One reason why they are so numerous is that the female usually remains in the den in winter, when the trapping season is on.

Because skunks kill so many insects and crop-destroying rodents, they are beneficial to man.

River Otter

Where are you most apt to find otters?

Their homes are close to, but not in, the water. In the summer, they are seldom seen on land. But in winter, they may go overland to reach another body of water. If they have been living in a pond, they may move to a river, where the water does not freeze to the bottom. In the very coldest climates, they search for places where waterfalls, rapids, or springs keep the water from freezing.

Otters have a large home territory. They may travel one hundred miles or more in search of a good place to live. Within this territory, the otter family follows definite trails.

What is unusual about the way otters get around?

They slide on their bellies a great deal—on ice, on snow, or on practically any smooth surface. To prepare for the slide, they make several jumps to gain momentum. They will even slide uphill on slopes that are not too steep.

What kind of den does an otter have?

The den is usually along the bank of a stream or lake. The entrance is most likely about four or five feet below the surface of the water. The tunnel then rises to a point above water level. Here the otter has a dry, comfortable home. Aboveground openings supply air.

Sometimes, a brushpile, a cavity at the base of a tree, a hollow log, or an abandoned beaver lodge or muskrat house will be used for a den. When trees are not available, a den may be made, wigwam fashion, by fastening marsh plants together.

A typical nest is made of sticks, shredded bark, leaves, and grass. It has a side chamber which serves as a toilet.

How do otters keep track of one another?

They have a pair of scent glands under the tail. They mark with scent such spots as their dens, their favorite sliding places, or areas where they roll in the grass after a swim. Otters are able to detect this scent and follow another otter's trail weeks later.

Members of an otter family feeding in the same general area make soft sounds to let one another know their locations.

What sounds do otters make?

They have a variety of happy and unhappy sounds. Normal conversation is carried on with a birdlike chirping or a chuckling sound. When pleased, they purr. They indicate alarm with a snort. Anger is expressed with a bark, a snarling growl, or a hiss. Pain is expressed with a scream.

Does the otter have any enemies?

Except for man, the otter has practically no enemies. The adults protect their young so well that they rarely fall victim to a predator. An adult otter can swim away from most of his enemies and is a savage fighter when cornered. He can usually escape a man by diving in and swimming underwater for some distance. In a fair fight with a dog, the dog will come out second-best.

In the winter, when pursued by a man or a dog on the snow, he may dive into a snowbank, tunnel through, and come up quite a distance away. He may also double back on his tracks to confuse his pursuer.

Does the father remain a part of the family after the young are born?

Apparently, the mother chases the father out of the den when the young are born. Later, when the youngsters are old enough to be out and around, the father is allowed to rejoin the group.

There are usually two to four young, born in the spring. When their eyes are open, the mother takes them to the water. She has to teach them to swim. Sometimes she takes them into the water on her back and dives out from under them, forcing them to swim for themselves. The parents teach the youngsters how to catch their food.

Why are otters fun to watch?

Because they are so playful, the old as well as the young. Otters are seldom seen alone. They enjoy rolling and frolicking together in the water and playing "ball" with suitable objects. These objects—pebbles, pieces of food, small sticks—are sometimes juggled on the nose in the manner of a trained circus performer. They also like to

play tag, follow the leader, or hide-and-seek with one another. The best-known game that otters have developed is that of "tobogganing" downhill. They like this game best when there is water at the end of the slide. Time after time, one after another, they will climb the hill for the sheer joy of coasting down it on their bellies.

If an otter cannot find someone to play with, he often plays by himself.

What do otters eat?

Primarily fish, which is why fishermen often dislike otters. However, most of the fish the otter eats are small and undesirable, and many are the kind that eat the eggs of game fish. So, in the long run, their presence may be beneficial to the fisherman. Otters also eat other meat. Poking their noses under submerged logs or rocks and digging in the mud with their paws, they find crayfish, shellfish, frogs, water beetles, and insects. They also on occasion eat muskrats, snakes, and waterfowl. Once in a while they seem to enjoy plant life such as pondweeds or blueberries.

How does the otter manage to catch a fish?

He is such a rapid and powerful swimmer that he can catch a fish, such as a trout or a salmon, by directly pursuing and outswimming it. His short legs, webbed feet, streamlined body, and powerful muscles all combine to make him fast and agile in the water.

How long can an otter stay underwater?

For three or four minutes. It can swim underwater nearly a quarter of a mile. Its nostrils and ears can be closed for underwater swimming.

How does the otter endure northern winters?

Otters have dense, oily fur, and a thick layer of fat beneath the skin to keep them warm. Their very active natures also help. And, in winter, after they have been swimming they send most of the water flying with a vigorous shake, or roll themselves dry in the snow.

Bobcat

Why is a bobcat sometimes called a "wildcat"?

Probably because when it is cornered, it looks and acts mean and wild. Its eyes blaze; it ruffles its fur; it snarls, hisses, spits, bares its teeth, and makes ugly faces.

A bobcat does not go around looking for fights, however. Its general reaction to danger is to slink away. It kills only to eat.

How big is a bobcat?

The average one is about twice the size and weight of an ordinary house cat. The largest on record weighed a whopping sixty-nine pounds.

How can you tell a bobcat from other wild cats?

The bobcat and the Canada lynx can be distinguished from other wild cats because they both have short tails,

tufts of hair on the ears, and "sideburns" (cheek whisk-ers). The bobcat is smaller than the lynx, has shorter ear tufts, and is much more spotted. There is a difference in the tip of the tail. That of the bobcat is black above, white below. The tip of the lynx's tail is completely encircled with black.

In what parts of the United States are bobcats found?

Their range includes the whole of the United States. They live in forests, mountainous regions, deserts, swamps, and rocky areas. Because they are very secretive and silent, they may be present in an area without humans being aware of them.

Can bobcats see in the dark?

Yes, but not in total blackness.

How does the bobcat keep its claws sharp?

Like all cats except the cheetah, the bobcat can pull his claws back into his paws. When he is walking, his claws are pulled in, and he walks on the pads of his feet. This not only gives him a more stealthy walk, but it saves wear and tear on the claws. He sharpens his claws now and them by scratching them on a tree.

What do bobcats eat?

They are meat eaters. Their food consists of rabbits, squirrels, woodchucks, cats, mice, and birds. They also kill fawns and adult deer that have been weakened by starvation or old age. Bobcats kill deer by sneaking up on them and leaping on their backs, sometimes from above.

They occasionally kill sheep and calves but are much more apt to attack animals on the open range than they are to come to farmyards in search of food.

Where does a bobcat have its den?

The preferred spot is under a rocky ledge or in a pile of rocks. If such a place is not available, the bobcat looks for a large tree cavity, a hollow stump, or a dense thicket. The den is lined with leaves or moss.

The young are born here in the spring. There are usually two or three in a litter. They are raised by the mother, who shows great affection for them. When the young ones are nearly weaned, the mother sometimes allows the father to come near again so that he can assist in obtaining food for them.

Is the bobcat a fast runner?

No. At best, he can do only twelve to fifteen miles an hour. When he is in a hurry, he has a bounding gallop. He can leap six to eight feet, perhaps even more, at a time.

Does the bobcat have any enemies?

Foxes, great horned owls, and cougars sometimes kill the young. Except for man, the adult has practically no enemies.

American Elk

Why is there confusion over the word "elk"?

The American elk is different from the European elk. A more proper name for the American elk is the Indian word "wapiti." But the word elk has been used for so many years to describe this animal, which is the second largest deer in America, that it is difficult to change now. The confusion arose because English settlers in Virginia thought the wapiti looked like the animal they called an elk (but which is really a moose).

Of what does an elk herd consist?

It depends on the time of year. In the fall, during the mating season, there are herds of bachelor bulls and there are harems. An elk harem is a herd that consists of one bull, as many cows as he can round up (sometimes thirty or more), and the offspring of those cows.

In winter, the small herds join together into large herds containing both sexes and all ages.

By late spring, the winter herds split up again into herds containing bulls and those containing cows. With the cows are their newborn calves and their year-old youngsters.

What is unusual about the way
elk care for their young?

They make use of baby-sitters! One or two mothers take charge and stay with the young ones while the other mothers in the herd wander away in search of food. If a predator, such as a coyote, comes along, the adults defend the young by striking at the preying animal with their hoofs. The hoofs of an elk are sharp, dangerous weapons.

The mother usually gives birth to only one calf at a time. The calf begins to eat vegetation soon after it joins the herd, a few days after birth. But it may not become completely weaned until late fall or even winter.

How many years does it take for
an elk to become mature?

Four or five years. When fully grown, a bull elk weighs an average of 700 to 800 pounds, a cow elk from 400 to 600 pounds. Six or seven years is the prime age for an elk.

How can you tell an elk from
a deer or a moose?

An elk can be quickly and positively identified by its large, conspicuous tan rump patch and matching tail. Elk are a great deal larger than deer.

The shape of the antlers helps distinguish the males of elk and moose. The elk's antlers are rounded and quite a bit like a deer's. Moose antlers are flattened, broad, and spoon-shaped.

All three of these animals belong to the deer family.

What do elk eat?

They like grass best and will eat it whenever it is available. When it is not, they eat weeds and the foliage and bark from shrubs and trees. If they are very hungry, elk will sometimes join cattle at the rancher's haystack.

What sounds do elk make?

The calves and their mothers make a squealing, bleating, or neighing sound when calling to one another. When they are alarmed, the calves make a sound like a shriek, and adults make a barking or a sharp snorting sound. During mating season, the males proclaim their presence with a long-drawn-out whistle called a "bugle." It is one of the most thrilling sounds in nature.

Does the elk have any enemies other than man?

Bears (both black and grizzly), bobcats, and coyotes sometimes kill elk calves for food. Adult elk can usually take care of themselves, either by running or by using their sharp hoofs as weapons. Elk have been known to kill coyotes, and, in at least one case, a bear. Wolves and cougars, on the other hand, can prey on adult elk as well as on young ones.

Do elk migrate?

Where the climate is severe, they do. They spend their winters in the foothills or valleys. As soon as the snow has melted sufficiently in the spring, they migrate up the mountains to their summer range. Here they stay until late fall.

Are elk plentiful in the United States today?

They occupy only a part of an area where they once were found in great numbers. They used to live in a good two-thirds of the United States. But they were overhunted for their meat, their hide, and their teeth, symbol of a fraternal organization. Conservationists realized that elk had been exterminated from ninety per cent of their range and campaigned to prevent them from becoming extinct. Elk were reintroduced into many areas. Today they can be found in mountainous and forested areas of western North America. In certain national parks, they have even become overcrowded.

White-Tailed Deer

What kind of family life do deer have?

The father takes no part in caring for the young. One or two fawns are born in the spring; occasionally there will be three. For the first few days, they hardly move. They remain close to the same spot for the first month; during this time, the mother comes to nurse them often. Then the young ones begin to follow the mother about as she feeds. A doe may stay with the mother for a year or so, but a young buck usually leaves after a few months.

Can you tell the age of a deer by its antlers?

You can get a rough idea. The first year, a buck usually has antlers with one or two spikes. Each year, until he is five, his antlers grow bigger, with more points. The most common number of points on the antlers of a mature deer is seven or eight, although there may be more. After a deer is about eight years old, the size of his antlers and the number of points decrease.

Other influences that determine antler size are heredity and the quantity and quality of food eaten. A reliable means of telling age is by examination of the deer's teeth.

What happens to deer antlers after they are shed?

Most are eaten by the deer themselves or by such creatures as squirrels, rabbits, porcupines, and mice. By gnawing the antlers, these animals obtain the calcium and other minerals they need. Antlers that are not eaten decay and eventually disappear.

How does a white-tailed deer signal
to other deer that danger is near?

When alarmed, a deer of this species raises its tail as it flees, and the white, fluffy underside is plainly visible. The tail is moved back and forth, like a white flag signaling danger.

What is the "velvet" of a deer's antlers?

It is a covering of thick skin with velvetlike hair that carries nourishment to the antlers. Antlers, which are grown only by the male, are shed each year—as are those

of the elk and the moose—and new ones start to grow in the spring. When growth has stopped, the velvet dries up and begins to peel. The deer speeds up the process by rubbing his antlers against tree trunks, often leaving scars on the trees. If you look for these scars, you may be able to tell if there are deer in the area. An easier indication to look for, however, is the presence of deer tracks (illustrated here).

What protection does a fawn have?

A young fawn is not strong enough to put up a fight, or fast enough to escape predators by fleeing. So it needs other means of protection. Its color is one of these means. Fawns are reddish-brown, dappled with white, and when they lie very still in the woods, they are extremely difficult to see. Also, fawns apparently have no odor the first few days of life, which protects them from predators that rely heavily on the sense of smell in finding victims. A dog will pass close by a young fawn and not know it is there.

What is a deer "yard"?

It is a place where a number of deer gather together to feed in winter. Such places can be recognized by the fact that the grass and weeds are trampled down. Deer are especially apt to yard when the snow is deep.

When deer gather in one spot, they often consume all available food in the area. Starvation for some of the deer results.

What do deer eat?

They prefer leaves and twigs of shrubs and trees. They do eat other things—herbs, grass, clover, legumes, mushrooms, mosses, lichens, and aquatic plants such as pond lilies. They are very fond of acorns. But during a winter starvation period, they will sometimes refuse to eat certain kinds of hay when it is put out for them.

How long do deer live?

In the wild, where it is hunted, a deer is not apt to live more than six years. But a life span of twenty or twenty-five years is possible; white-tails have lived that long in parks, where they were protected from danger. Apparently, deer sometimes die from a combination of fear and exhaustion. Biologists tell of deer that have died as a result of being chased by snowmobiles.

How fast can a white-tailed deer run?

A top speed of fifty miles an hour has been reported for white-tails. A more normal running speed is thirty miles an hour. A deer's gallop is different from that of a horse. It consists of three or four bounds followed by a leap, which can be from ten to twenty feet. From a standing position, a deer can leap over an object seven or eight feet high.

Are white-tailed deer in danger of becoming extinct?

No. The white-tail is believed to be more numerous now than it was in Colonial days. In some areas, it has become overly abundant. One reason for this is that many of the deer's enemies, such as the mountain lion and the wolf, have been greatly reduced in numbers by man. Another reason is that man's timber cutting results in the type of habitat where deer thrive. The shrubs and young trees that grow up afterward are what deer like best.

Are deer always gentle?

No. Does and young deer are almost always gentle, but an old buck during the mating season can be ugly-tempered and on the lookout for a fight.

Moose

*In what type of area will you be most
likely to see a moose?*

Moose are found in evergreen forests of northern
United States, Alaska, and Canada. Their favorite haunts
are in open places near water or marshland. They eat the
twigs and bark of the willow, maple, birth, aspen, fir, and
cottonwood trees which grow in such places. In summer,
they eat many of the plants found in lakes or swamps;
they are especially fond of duckweeds and water lilies.

When danger threatens, moose retreat to the dense evergreen forests, bordering these open places.

How big is a moose?

It is the largest animal with antlers that has ever lived on earth. A full-grown bull moose can weigh as much as 1,500 pounds throughout most of its range. Eighteen hundred pounds is the reported maximum from Alaska. The female is somewhat smaller. The antlers of a mature bull moose may be over six feet from tip to tip and weigh as much as eighty-five pounds.

At Isle Royale in Lake Superior, where there are a great many moose, your chances of seeing one are excellent. When a big bull moose steps onto the trail in front of you (and this is quite apt to happen), its size is *most* impressive!

What is the "bell" of a moose?

It is a flap of skin that hangs from the neck. It varies in size, with twelve to fifteen inches being average. All moose —young and old, male and female—have bells. No one has yet discovered what purpose it serves.

Why do moose sometimes eat bare earth?

Some earth is very high in mineral compounds, including salt. Moose, as well as other hoofed animals, often eat this mineral-rich earth in spring and early summer. It probably acts as a "spring tonic," something the body needs for maximum health.

How do moose get rid of insects?

Flies and mosquitoes bother moose a great deal. To get rid of them, a moose will sometimes stand in water deep enough almost to cover him. Another technique is to roll in the mud. Under a layer of mud, the skin is protected from fly and mosquito bites.

What is the "rutting season"?

This is the mating season. The term is used not only for moose but for many other animals as well.

The cow moose gives a low, hoarse call during the rutting season. Bulls challenge one another with hoarse bellows, whistles, and grunts. The rutting season lasts from about mid-September to mid-October.

The whistle of certain diesel locomotives sounds a good deal like a moose call. As a result, a bull moose will occasionally attack a train and get himself killed.

How does the mother moose protect her young?

If an enemy comes close to the calf, the mother stretches her head forward—the hairs of her mane on end—lays back her ears, and snorts as a horse would do. She may then rear on her hind legs and paw the air. If this doesn't scare away the intruder, she stamps her feet. If all warnings fail, she comes bounding toward the enemy. Her sharp front hoofs are dangerous weapons. A mother moose defending her young has been known to chase a black bear up a tree.

How long does the moose calf stay with its mother?

A young moose is usually weaned when it is about six to eight weeks old. But the youngster remains with his mother until he is almost a year old. By then, the mother is usually about to give birth again. She drives the yearling away. A moose calf apparently has a difficult time getting used to the idea that its mother doesn't want it around any more. It looks and acts very forlorn during this period.

How long do moose live?

They can live as long as twenty-two years, but very few live longer than fifteen or twenty years. Man and wolves are about the only enemies they have, although bears and coyotes sometimes kill the calves.

*What should you do if a moose starts
running toward you in the wild?*

Climb a tree or run for your car, if it is nearby. Moose are ordinarily inclined to ignore humans—at a reasonable distance. But a bull moose during the rutting season, and a cow moose with a calf, may attack humans.

Pronghorn (Antelope)

How does a pronghorn signal danger?

A pronghorn has a large white patch on each buttock. The long hairs on these patches are raised in response to fear or excitement. Then two brilliant white rosettes are displayed. In bright sunlight, these rosettes are visible a couple of miles away. They show up when the rest of the animal cannot be seen. This serves as a warning to other pronghorns to be on guard.

At the same time the rump patches are raised, a musky odor is released. This can be smelled far away. It too is a danger signal.

How fast can the pronghorn run?

For short stretches, sixty miles an hour is a conservative figure. Although it cannot continue this speed very long, it can run several miles at forty miles an hour. It is the fastest mammal on the North American continent.

Pronghorns have a curious habit of running parallel to a car or a man on horseback for some distance. They then pull ahead and cross in front, as if to prove that they have won the race.

What natural enemies does the pronghorn have?

The wolf and the coyote are the only animals that try to catch a full-grown pronghorn. In addition, golden eagles, bears, and foxes go after the fawns.

How can a wolf or a coyote catch a pronghorn?

The pronghorn can run faster, of course, but coyotes and wolves sometimes run in relays. In this way, they tire the pronghorn until one of them is able to catch it.

Why were pronghorns easy for hunters to kill?

They have a strong sense of curiosity. Indians used to lure them close by waving pieces of cloth for them to wonder about. Throughout the years, hunters have lured pronghorns to their deaths by such devices as lying on their backs and kicking their legs in the air, or have crept close beneath a sheet or a buffalo robe.

The pronghorns of today, though, have learned to be more cautious.

On which of its senses does
the pronghorn depend most?

Sight. Pronghorns have large eyes and a wide angle of vision. Man needs an eight-power telescope for comparable vision.

Do pronghorns form harems?

Yes. The male pronghorn, like the male elk, gathers together as large a herd of females as he can manage. Most pronghorn bucks seem satisfied with three or four does, but there may be as many as fifteen in a harem.

How does the mother protect her fawns?

She stays away from them, except to nurse them. Like young deer, young pronghorns have practically no scent. When flattened on the ground, they are very inconspicuous. Usually, there are twins. The mother goes a short distance from the herd, gives birth to one young, then goes about a hundred yards away and gives birth to another. In this way, she separates the fawns, so that a predator can't attack two fawns at once.

If a predator comes too close to a fawn, the fawn jumps up and runs. It can run twenty-five miles an hour after the first day or so. The mother comes into the action when the fawn begins to run. She goes after a small predator, butts him with her horns, and strikes at him with her front hoofs. Neither a fox nor a lone coyote cares to tangle with a protective mother pronghorn. If the predator is too large for her to fight, she tries to lure him into chasing her.

When the fawns are a few days old, they join the herd.

What do pronghorns eat?

They feed on shrubs, sagebrush, Russian thistle, greasewood, cactus, and grass. They also like alfalfa and oats, and are sometimes a nuisance to farmers. Although they are perfectly capable of leaping over fences, they prefer to crawl through or under them.

Pronghorns can go for months, possibly a lifetime, without drinking water. They obtain the needed moisture from plants.

How do pronghorns manage to survive severe winters?

Not all of them do survive, but their fur is designed to provide maximum protection. It consists of thick, tubular hairs that have large air cells which serve as insulation.

In winter, pronghorns seek more sheltered areas. They may come to a lower altitude or a wooded valley, seeking places where the snow is not too deep. Even so, many thousands may die in an especially severe winter. Deep snow prevents them from getting to their food. It also aids their enemies. Wolves and coyotes are able to drive the pronghorns into snowdrifts and kill them there without difficulty.

*Why is the pronghorn not considered
a true antelope?*

The horns of the pronghorn are hollow, like those of antelope, but differ in two ways. First, each horn has a spike, or prong. Second, the outer sheath of the horn is shed and renewed each year. True antelope keep the entire horn for life. The pronghorn is placed in a family all by itself.

Where are pronghorns found today?

They are found in open prairies, upland plains, and the sagebrush plains of western United States, where the land has not been taken over by farmers or ranchers. Before the arrival of the white man, there were at least thirty or forty million of these graceful animals in North America. According to some, pronghorns were as numerous as buffalo, perhaps even more numerous. Now there are about 400,000. The number seems to be holding fairly constant, thanks to conservation efforts.

American Buffalo (Bison)

*Why do scientists prefer the name
"bison" to "buffalo"?*

They reserve the term "buffalo" for the water buffalo
of Asia and the African buffalo. The true buffalo is not
humpbacked, as our American buffalo is. However, as
with so many terms, the use of "buffalo" for "bison" is so
common that it is very difficult to change at this point.

Are buffaloes slow, clumsy animals?

No. They can run at speeds of up to thirty-five miles an
hour and can wheel about with amazing agility. They also

manage to climb up and down mountainsides so steep that a horse and rider must use switchbacks to cover the same ground. There is an annual roundup of buffalo at the National Bison Range in Montana. Men assigned to handle this roundup often find the buffaloes are very nimble and skillful at escaping capture.

Are buffaloes dangerous?

Yes. They are unpredictable and dangerous. Even a buffalo that has been domesticated since birth may suddenly attack a man for no reason at all and kill him. It's a good idea to have a strong fence or a safe distance between you and a buffalo, or to have your car handy for retreat. A number of buffalo observers have saved themselves from a charging buffalo by climbing a tree.

Why do buffaloes look so front-heavy?

Partly, it's because the buffalo has a massive head, humped shoulders, and small hindquarters. The front-heavy effect is exaggerated because the fur on the front part of the body is long and shaggy, while that beyond the shoulders is so short it looks clipped by comparison.

*Why do railroad tracks and highways
often follow buffalo trails?*

Surveyors discovered that the buffalo usually followed the easiest of all possible routes. When traveling to new grazing grounds or to water, buffaloes often moved single file, creating a definite trail. These trails crossed the prairie, forded wide rivers, and climbed mountain passes. Humans following these trails found that the buffalo forded rivers at places where there was easy access and shallow water. In most cases, the buffalo chose the easiest grade and the best mountain passes. Not being able to improve on the buffalo's skill as a pathfinder, the surveyors took advantage of it.

How do buffaloes get their food and water in winter?

A buffalo will push its nose through the snow and swing his head from side to side. This action creates a clearing of uncovered grass. The buffalo eats, then clears another section in the same way. Even snow four feet deep can be pushed away in this manner. Most grazing animals use their paws instead of their heads to clear away the snow.

If there is a layer of ice over the water, a thirsty buffalo breaks through the ice with blows of the head.

How did it happen that buffaloes would follow one another blindly over a cliff?

Buffaloes do not rate highly in intelligence; however, it was force of numbers rather than sheer stupidity that caused these catastrophes. Stampedes would start when one or more leaders began to run, sometimes for no apparent reason. Once the leaders started to run, the herd followed. Then the leaders could not stop, or even turn aside. They were pushed forward by the mass of those behind. The buffaloes behind could not see the danger. And so a whole herd might tumble over a steep cliff or become mired in quicksand.

Why were so many telegraph poles knocked over by buffaloes?

Buffaloes like to rub their shoulders against trees or boulders. The action probably relieves itching, tension, or both. So when man began to string telegraph wires across the plains, the buffaloes were delighted. The poles on which the wires were strung made excellent rubbing posts. Since buffaloes can weigh up to 3,000 pounds, they knocked over some of the poles in their exuberance. To discourage this activity, men added spikes to the poles. The buffalo liked the spiked poles even better than the plain ones.

The problem was short-lived, however, since buffaloes were soon practically exterminated by hunting.

What are buffalo wallows?

Buffaloes frequently paw up the sod, roll on their backs, and take a dust bath. This act is called wallowing. The resulting patches of bare earth are called buffalo wallows. Some of these saucer-shaped depressions are fifteen feet across, or even more.

Prairie dog towns used to be a favorite spot for such wallowing. The buffalo arose feeling better, no doubt. But the poor prairie dogs, whose homes had been disturbed, were not so happy.

One theory is that buffaloes wallow to relieve itching caused by flies, mosquitoes, and parasites. A more recent theory, and one that seems to explain observed facts more adequately, is that a wallowing buffalo is expressing tension or conflict.

Where are the young born?

Usually, a buffalo cow goes a short distance from the herd to give birth. She licks her calf, sniffs it, and nuzzles it. This is necessary so that she and her calf will recognize one another when they rejoin the herd two or three days later. The calf nurses until its mother weans it the following winter.

Did the buffalo have enemies other than man?

Wolves, bears, cougars, and coyotes picked off the young, weak, or wounded buffaloes. Until the white man and his gun came along, even man was no great threat to survival of the buffalo. But the white hunter killed just for "sport." At other times, he took the hide, or killed for the sake of the tongue, which sold for twenty-five cents! There were at least sixty million buffalo when white men began hunting them in earnest. One herd seen in 1871 was twenty-five miles wide and fifty miles deep. By 1900, only three hundred were left in the United States.

Why were the plains Indians so
dependent on the buffalo?
    The buffalo provided them with almost everything they needed. The flesh provided them with food; the skin with a tepee, blankets, clothing, roundboats, and war shields; the bones were used for scrapers; the ribs served as runners for sleds; the stomach provided a storage container for food; the hair was braided into ropes. Buffalo horns were made into spoons and bows. Buffalo "chips," which resemble "cow pies," made good fuel for a fire when there was no wood handy. Even the tail was used—for swatting flies.

Are there many buffaloes
in the United States today?
    There are a few hundred roaming free in Alaska, Arizona, and Utah. The rest are in private herds, zoos, national parks, and wildlife refuges.

Mountain Goat

*Why do biologists still have much
to learn about mountain goats?*

These goats are usually found above the treeline in steep, rocky mountain areas. They can stand severe winter conditions that man finds difficult to endure. As a result, not much is known about the life of mountain goats in winter. Their thick, fleecy undercoat, with its layer of long, shaggy guard hairs, protects them from the strong winds and extremely low temperatures of their mountain-peak homeland.

Goats are rarely ever seen. Your best chances to spot one are in the mountains of Washington, Montana, Idaho, or Alaska.

Is the mountain goat really a goat?

No, it is not a true goat. It has features of both goat and antelope and is sometimes referred to as a goat antelope. Its neck and shoulders are heavier than those of a goat, and its horns do not twist into spirals as do a goat's.

How are goats able to climb cliffs that
are almost straight up and down?

Their toes act like pliers. They can spread their two toes apart and then pull them together tightly over the rocks. The soft pads in between act as suction cups. Mountain goats are the most sure-footed large animals on the North American continent.

A goat is able to stand up on his hind legs, place his front legs on a ledge five or six feet above him, and pull his body up to the higher ledge with a shimmying motion. He can also stand up on his hind legs and turn himself about on a narrow ledge.

The belief that a goat never falls is incorrect. Falls seldom occur but have been known to happen.

Do goats ever hurry?

They rarely run or jump as sheep do. Even when they are escaping from danger, they usually move at a fast, stiff-legged walk instead of running. Their ability to climb in places where no other animal can follow apparently makes running an art seldom needed. They can, however, jump twelve feet or so, if necessary.

What enemies do mountain goats have?

Mountain lions, bobcats, bears, wolves, coyotes, and eagles occasionally manage to kill a kid. The adults will often successfully defy the attempts of eagles to take a kid. One observer tells of four adults forming a circle around two kids, protecting them with their horns from an attack by two eagles. Another tells of a nanny standing on her hind legs and striking out with her horns whenever an eagle swooped down near her kid. The eagle gave up.

Healthy adults are seldom attacked, except when they come down the mountain slopes and into the valleys for food or to visit a salt lick. The greatest dangers for mountain goats come from the environment. Severe winter weather and lack of food cause many to die. In the spring, they may be killed by avalanches.

How do mountain goats fight?

They fight with their horns, but they do not rush at each other headlong, as do most other animals that battle with their horns. Mountain goats circle each other, each one trying to jab the other in the chest or belly. They don't fight very often; in a confrontation, a mountain goat is more apt to try to bluff his opponent than to fight him.

How soon is the kid able to stand on its feet?

Almost immediately after birth, the kid stands up and begins to nurse. Half an hour after birth, he may be jumping about. His nanny keeps him hidden for a few days, then both join a band of other nannies and their offspring. The bond between nanny and kid is close. Even when the kid is a year old, he may still follow his mother and be protected by her.

Which has the more dangerous horns— bighorn sheep or mountain goats?

Mountain goats. Although the horns of a bighorn sheep weigh sixty-five to ninety times as much, the horns of the goat are much more dangerous. They have been known to kill grizzly bears.

How do goats guard against danger?

Both mountain goats and bighorn sheep have sentinels on guard to watch for danger while the rest of the herd feeds. Bighorn sheep depend primarily on their keen eyesight to detect danger. Goats, however, depend more on their sense of smell than on sight or hearing.

What do mountain goats eat?

To a casual observer, it would seem that on the steep mountain cliffs where these goats live, there is very little food. However, lichens, mosses, grass, twigs, and leaves of small shrubs provide the needed food.

Are mountain goats in danger of becoming extinct?

No. They have not been overhunted, partly because their horns do not tempt trophy hunters as much as do those of the bighorn sheep. Their choice of a rugged and isolated homeland results in their being hunted only by the most ambitious. Attempts to stock them in new areas and to restock them in areas where they were once plentiful have been very successful.

Bighorn Sheep

*Do the horns of the male sheep
serve any purpose?*

Yes. The ram's horns are used as a weapon in attack
and as a shield for defense. They are also a status symbol.
The ram with the largest horns is most likely to come out
on top in the battles that occur between mature rams during the rutting season. In this way, he establishes himself
as the leader.

*Do rams with the largest horns
usually live the longest?*

No. The life expectancy is less than average for the ram with the largest horns. He is the one challenged by any ram who would like to take over as leader. As a result, he has to fight many duels. Injury and exhaustion reduce his life span.

Sheep in the wild seldom live to be more than fourteen years old.

How large are the horns of the bighorn?

The largest horns officially recorded measured forty-nine and one-half inches, from base to tip, on the outside curve. The average weight of upper skull and horns on adult rams is about twenty-five pounds. That's a pretty heavy headpiece to carry about while climbing up and down mountains!

How do young rams get practice in using their horns?

At an early age, they start to play "king of the mountain." One young ram gets on top of a rock and challenges all comers. When he is pushed off, another takes his place. This is play, but it is also preparation for the day when the young ram will challenge an older one to a duel.

*Can you tell the age of sheep by
the size of their horns?*

Yes. Like trees, sheep horns have rings marking periods of growth and rest. Lines indicate lack of growth during winter months. These lines grow closer together as the years go by. After about ten years, they are so close together it is hard to count them. Wear and tear on the horn tips also makes it difficult to tell the exact age of an old ram. Most rams past their prime have broken tips.

Females also have horns, but they remain small and only slightly curved.

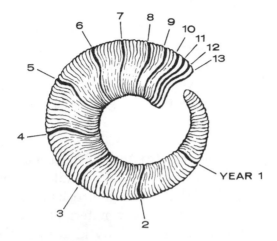

How do sheep survive the cold winter?

They put on extra layers of fat before winter sets in. This and their heavy coats (which are not wool, but hair, as those of deer) insulate them from the cold. When resting in cold weather, they bunch their feet beneath their bodies for warmth. They also conserve energy by avoiding snow that is too deep or has a crust which they would break through. They search for areas where the wind or the sun has cleared away much of the snow.

When caught in a bad winter storm, they may seek shelter, huddling close together against a cliff, or they may retreat to caves in the area.

What do bighorns eat?

They are much more particular about what they eat than are goats, elk, or deer. In mountain areas, ninety-five per cent of their diet consists of tender grasses. They eat only the flowers of certain herbs. Salt licks attract them. In summer, they find their food in meadows at high altitudes. In winter, they migrate down into the valleys.

Desert bighorns have had to adapt to a shortage of grass. They eat mountain mahogany, acacia, buckbrush, and various cacti.

Do bighorns ever make a noise?

Yes, although they are usually silent animals. Lambs and their mothers make a "baaa" sound. Snorts are used to warn one another of danger, and grunts or snorts are used by the rams when they are fighting. Rams also grind their teeth loudly when angry and sometimes growl when they are kicking.

How do bighorns manage to climb such sheer cliffs?

They are well equipped for the job. Like the mountain goat, they have toes that pinch the rocks beneath. Their hoofs are covered with an elastic material that absorbs the shock of landing and can grip any kind of surface, as a suction cup does.

Although a cliff may appear to be perfectly sheer and smooth, it invariably has small ledges and crevices on its surface—and a bighorn sheep needs only a two-inch foothold to climb a cliff. He climbs, not slowly and methodically as a mountain goat does, but by leaps and bounds. He can jump straight up six or seven feet in one bound. As he climbs, he zigzags from one foothold to another.

How do bighorns come down sheer cliffs?

Coming down safely is harder than going up, as many of us have discovered from experience. People who have seen bighorns successfully descending almost vertical cliffs describe the movement as half leaping, half falling. They can cover twenty feet at a time in a downward leap. To break their speed, they bounce from one small footrest to another. The final leap sometimes looks almost like a dive, but the animal lands on his feet, using his joints to provide a springing action which serves as a shock absorber.

Sometimes a bighorn will descend by leaping from one side of a crevasse to another.

Where are the young born?

The mother leaves the band when she begins to feel birth pangs. She goes a short distance away—behind some rocks, or in a brush-sheltered hollow. There she gives birth to one or perhaps two young. After about a week, mother and lamb rejoin the flock of ewes, lambs, and year-old rams. The lamb will be weaned at about four to six months. If it is a male, he will stay with the same flock until he becomes mature enough to join a separate band of young rams. The bachelor band ignores the band of ewes and their young except during November and December—the mating season.

If the lamb is a female, she will remain with the original flock.

Why are there so few bighorns in the
United States today?

Bighorns attract hunters because their horns make fine trophies and their flesh is good to eat. As a result, they have been overhunted. The amount of land where bighorns can graze without competition from cattle is continually diminishing. Another factor in their decline is that they catch diseases introduced by domestic sheep.

Biologists fear that bighorns are on the verge of becoming extinct. They exist only in a few scattered wilderness areas. Hunting, legal and illegal, threatens even these remnants of an animal that was once plentiful.

Bibliography

Bailey, Theodore N., "The Elusive Bobcat." *Natural History*, Vol. 81 (October, 1972), pp. 42–49.

Barkalow, Frederick S., Jr., and Monica Shorten, *The World of the Gray Squirrel*. Philadelphia and New York: J. B. Lippincott Co., 1973.

Barker, Will, *Familiar Animals of America*. New York: Harper & Brothers, 1956.

Bartlett, Des, and Jen Barlett, "Nature's Aquatic Engineers—Beavers." *National Geographic*, Vol. 145 (May, 1974), pp. 716–32.

Bere, Rennie, *Antelopes*. New York: Arco Publishing Co., 1970.

Booth, Ernest S., *How to Know the Mammals*. Dubuque, Iowa: Wm. C. Brown Co., 1971.

Breland, Osmond P., *Animal Life and Lore*. New York: Harper & Row, 1963.

Bueler, Lois E., *Wild Dogs of the World*. New York: Stein and Day, 1973.

Burt, William H., *A Field Guide to the Mammals*. Boston: Houghton Mifflin Co., 1964.

Buyukmihci, Hope Sawyer, *Hour of the Beaver*. New York: Rand McNally Co., 1971.

Cahalane, Victor H., *Mammals of North America*. New York: The Macmillan Co., 1961.

———, ed., *Alive in the Wild*. Englewood Cliffs, N.J.: Prentice-Hall Inc., 1970.

Clark, James L. *The Great Arc of the Wild Sheep*. Norman, Oklahoma: University of Oklahoma Press, 1964.

Clement, Roland C., *Hammond Nature Atlas*. Maplewood, N.J.: The Ridge Press, Inc., and Hammond, Inc., 1973.

Costello, David F., *The World of the Prairie Dog*. Philadelphia and New York: J. B. Lippincott Co., 1970.

Devoe, Alan, *The Fascinating Animal World*. New York: McGraw-Hill Book Co., 1951.

Drimmer, Frederick, ed.-in-chief. *The Animal Kingdom*, Vols. 1 and 2. Garden City, N.Y.: Doubleday and Co., 1954.

Garretson, Martin S., *A Short History of the American Bison*. Freeport, N.Y.: Books for Libraries Press, 1971.

Geist, Valerius, *Mountain Sheep, a Study in Behavior and Evolution*. Chicago: University of Chicago Press, 1971.

George, Jean Craighead, *Beastly Inventions*. New York: Van Rees Press, 1970.

Grzimek, Bernhard, *Grzimek's Animal Encyclopedia*. Vols. 10 and 13. New York: Van Nostrand Reinhold Co., 1972.

Gustavson, Carl L., and others, "Predator Control by Aversive Conditioning." *Science*, Vol. 184 (May 3, 1974), pp. 581–83.

Henisch, B. A., and H. K. Henisch, *Chipmunk Portrait*. State College, Penn.: The Carnation Press, 1970.

Ingles, Lloyd G., *Mammals of the Pacific States*. Stanford, Calif.: Stanford University Press, 1965.

Jackson, Hartley H., *Mammals of Wisconsin*. Madison, Wis.: University of Wisconsin Press, 1961.

Keefe, James F., *The World of the Opossum*. Philadelphia and New York: J. B. Lippincott Co., 1967.

MacClintock, Dorcas, *Squirrels of North America*. New York: Van Nostrand Reinhold Co., 1970.

Mason, George F., *Animal Homes*. New York: William Morrow and Co., 1947.

Matthews, L. Harrison, ed., *The Life of Mammals*. London: Wiedenfeld and Nicolson, 1969.

McHugh, Tom, *The Time of the Buffalo*. New York: Alfred A. Knopf, 1972.

McNulty, Faith, *Must They Die?* Garden City, N.Y.: Doubleday and Co., 1971.

Mech, L. David, "A New Profile for the Wolf." *Natural History*, Vol. 83 (April, 1974), pp. 26–31.

Mellanby, Kenneth, *The Mole*. New York: Taplinger Publishing Co., 1973.

Morgan, James K., "Last Stand for the Bighorn." *National Geographic*, Vol. 144 (September, 1973), pp. 383–99.

——, "Bighorn Profile" *Audubon*, Vol. 75 (November, 1973), pp. 4–15.

——, "Slamming the Ram into Oblivion." *Audubon*, Vol. 75 (November, 1973), pp. 16–19.

Morris, Desmond, *The Mammals*. New York and Evanston, Ill.: Harper & Row, 1965.

National Geographic Society, *Wild Animals of North America*. Washington, D.C.: Book Service, 1960.

——, *The Marvels of Animal Behavior*, Washington, D.C.: Book Service, 1972.

Orr, Robert T., *Mammals of North America*. New York: Doubleday and Co., 1971.

Park, Ed, *The World of the Bison*. Philadelphia and New York: J. B. Lippincott Co., 1969.

Park, Ed, *The World of the Otter*. Philadelphia and New York: J. B. Lippincott Co., 1971.

Perry, Richard, *Bears*. New York: Arco Publishing Co., 1970.

Peterson, Randolph L., *The Mammals of Eastern Canada*. Toronto: Oxford University Press, 1966.

Prince, J. H., *Animals in the Night—Senses in Action After Dark*. New York: Thomas Nelson Co., 1968.

Rood, Ronald, *Animals Nobody Loves*. Brattleboro, Vt.: The Stephen Greene Press, 1971.

Rue, Leonard Lee, *The World of the Beaver*. Philadelphia and New York: J. B. Lippincott Co., 1964.

—— *The World of the Red Fox*. Philadelphia and New York: J. B. Lippincott Co., 1969.

Rutter, Russel, and Douglas H. Pimlot, *The World of the Wolf*. Philadelphia and New York: J. B. Lippincott Co., 1968.

Schoonmaker, W. J., *The World of the Woodchuck*. Philadelphia and New York: J. B. Lippincott Co., 1966.

Seton, Ernest Thompson, *Lives of Game Animals*. Vol. I–IV. Garden City, N.Y.: Doubleday, Doran and Co., 1929.

Stenlund, Milt, "Trials of the Timber Wolf," *The Minnesota Volunteer*, Vol. 37 (March–April, 1974), pp. 51–61.

Tee-Van, Helen Damrosch, *Small Mammals Are Where You Find Them*. New York: Alfred A. Knopf, Inc., 1966.

U.S. Department of the Interior, *Threatened Wildlife of the United States*, 1973 Edition. Washington, D.C.: U.S. Government Printing Office, 1973.

Van Wormer, Joe, *The World of the Coyote*. Philadelphia and New York: J. B. Lippincott Co., 1964.

——, *The World of the Black Bear*. Philadelphia and New York: J. B. Lippincott Co., 1966.

——, *The World of the American Elk*. Philadelphia and New York: J. B. Lippincott Co., 1969.

——, *The World of the Moose*. Philadelphia and New York: J. B. Lippincott Co., 1972.

——, *The World of the Pronghorn*. Philadelphia and New York: J. B. Lippincott, Co., 1969.

Verts, B. J., *The Biology of the Striped Skunk*. Urbana, Ill.: University of Illinois Press, 1967.

Whitehead, G. Kenneth, *Deer of the World*. New York: Viking Press, 1972.

Young, Stanley P., *The Bobcat of North America*. Harrisburg, Pa.: The Stackpole Co. and The Wildlife Management Institute, 1958.

Glossary

The animals described in this book are listed here with information concerning their appearance, size, and the habitat and areas in continental United States where they may be found. In addition, some of the more technical terms used in the book are defined.

AMERICAN ELK, see **ELK, AMERICAN**

ANTELOPE, see **PRONGHORN**

BADGER   A short-legged, heavy-bodied animal that has a squat, flattened look. The fur is a grizzled brownish gray. A white stripe runs from the nose over the head. The cheeks are white with a long black spot. Length, including tail, is from two to two and one-half feet. Weight is from twelve to twenty-four pounds. Badgers are night creatures but may be seen in the evening or early morning. They are great diggers and prefer open grasslands and deserts. Badgers are found in the western two-thirds of the United States, with the exception of Alaska.

BEAR, BLACK   A medium-sized bear that can be black, brown, or almost white. There is usually a white spot on the chest. It is the most common bear in the United States and is usually harmless though a half-tame bear or a mother with cubs may become violent if provoked. The black bear stands about two to three feet tall at the shoulders and has a total length of five to six feet. The weight varies from 200 to 500 pounds. It is found in swampy areas of Florida and Louisiana, in the Great Smoky Mountains, in most of the northern tier of states, and in the mountains of the West.

BEAVER The largest rodent in our country, the beaver is dark brown with short legs, large webbed hind feet, and a scaly paddle-shaped tail. Beavers are found only in or near the water. Your best chance of seeing one is in the evening. The average beaver is three to four feet in total length and weighs forty to sixty pounds. Except for Florida, Nevada, and parts of southern California, beavers are found throughout the United States.

BIGHORN, see SHEEP, BIGHORN

BIOLOGIST A person who studies plants and animals and their life processes.

BISON, see BUFFALO, AMERICAN

BLACK BEAR, see BEAR, BLACK

BOBCAT The bobcat looks like an overgrown house cat with a bobbed tail. It has short ear tufts that may be only barely visible. Its tail is black on the upper surface of the tip and white on the bottom. Unlike the lynx's, the bobcat's short fur is brownish rather than gray and is much more spotted. Bobcats are from thirty-two to forty-two inches in length and weigh about seventeen pounds, though they may be three or four times as heavy. They hunt mostly at night and are found in rocky areas, swamps, and forests. Although we seldom see them, bobcats live throughout most of the United States and continue to hold their own in spite of persecution by man.

BUFFALO, AMERICAN (BISON) A very large animal with humped shoulders, massive head, short curved horns, and a beard. It has long, shaggy brown hair on the head, shoulders, and front legs. The hair on the rest of the body is very short. The buffalo is five to six feet tall at the shoulders and is ten to twelve and one-half feet in length. Males weigh as much as a ton; cows are much smaller, 700 to 900 pounds. Buffalo, once very abundant in the plains, are now found almost exclusively in zoos and parks.

CHIPMUNK Chipmunks are small, striped squirrels that are usually seen scampering about on the ground or sitting on their haunches eating. They are active in the daytime. They have stripes on the head as well as on the back and are grayish or reddish brown in color. Total length is from seven to eleven inches, weight from one to five ounces. Eastern chipmunks are found in suburban areas and deciduous forests in most of the eastern states. There are sixteen species of western chipmunks, found in eleven western states.

COTTONTAIL, see **RABBIT, COTTONTAIL**

COYOTE The coyote, also called prairie wolf or brush wolf, looks like a medium-sized dog. It is gray or reddish gray, with a more pointed nose and a bushier tail than most dogs. It is much larger than a fox and much smaller than a timber wolf. Total length is forty-two to fifty inches. Weight is twenty to thirty pounds on the average, occasionally as heavy as sixty pounds. Coyotes like prairies, open woodlands, and brushy areas, and are usually out only at night. They are found in most parts of the country except the Southeast.

DEER, WHITE-TAILED When we speak of a "deer," we usually mean the white-tailed variety, because is it so abundant and well known. Its coat is reddish in summer, grayish in winter. The upper surface of the tail is the color of the body, and the lower surface is white; the tail may be raised and waved like a flag to signal danger. The antlers of the buck consist of a main beam with prongs branching from it. The buck is three or three and one-half feet tall at the shoulders and weighs from 75 to 400 pounds. The doe is smaller. White-tailed deer may be seen in forests, swamps, or brushy areas, usually in the morning or in the evening, in practically every part of the country.

ELK, AMERICAN (WAPITI) Larger than a deer, the elk has a reddish brown body and a conspicuous tan or yellowish rump patch. Males have antlers that may have a spread of five feet or more. They also have a distinctive neck mane. Their height at the shoulders is four to five feet, and their weight runs from 700 to 1,000 pounds. Females are smaller. They are found in mountainous areas of the West, in alpine meadows in summer and in valleys in winter.

EVOLUTION A theory that various types of animals are the distant relatives of other animals that existed earlier in history. The differences between the current forms and the earlier forms are due to modifications over many generations.

EXTINCT An animal that is no longer in existence, such as the dodo bird.

FLYING SQUIRREL, see **SQUIRREL, FLYING**

FOX, RED   About the size of a small collie, the red fox rarely weighs more than twelve pounds. Its total length is three to three and one-half feet, nearly half of which is tail. The red fox is usually reddish yellow with various amounts of black, but its color may vary from black to silvery gray, or be a mixture of reddish yellow and a darker color. The long, bushy tail is always tipped with white. Feet and lower legs are black. The red fox likes a mixture of forest and open country, and is most active at night, in early morning, or in late evening. It is found over most of the United States.

GOAT, MOUNTAIN   A shaggy white coat, a beard, smooth black horns that curve slightly backward, humped shoulders, and black hoofs make the mountain goat easy to identify. Its height at the shoulders is three or three and one-half feet; it weighs from 150 to 300 pounds. It can be spotted in mountainous areas, usually on rocky crags above the timberline. Mountain goats are far from plentiful, but you may be able to see them in the Black Hills, in Alaska or in the following national parks: Mount Rainier, Olympic, Glacier.

GOPHER, POCKET   Small to medium-sized rodents, pocket gophers are usually brown but may vary from nearly white to nearly black. They have external fur-lined cheek pouches on each side of the mouth. Their incisor teeth are large and yellowish and are on the outside when the mouth is closed. Eyes and ears are small. Their soft fur lies close to the body, but it cannot be brushed equally well in any direction, as a mole's can. You can tell if there is a pocket gopher around by the fan-shaped piles of earth it throws out from its tunnel. Gophers are from seven to fourteen inches in length and weigh from two and one-half to eighteen ounces. There are a number of different species. They are found in southeastern, central and western United States.

GRAY SQUIRREL, see **SQUIRREL, GRAY**

HIBERNATE   To pass the winter in a semisleep, during which the animal consumes little food and his bodily functions slow down.

LITTER   The offspring of an animal at one birth.

MAMMAL   An animal, such as man, that nourishes its young with milk from the mammary glands of the female. Usually the skin of mammals is covered with hair.

MARSUPIAL A mammal, such as an opossum or a kangaroo, that has a pouch on the abdomen in which the young are carried and nursed. (Only the females have pouches.)

MINK Famous for the beauty of its fur, the mink is about the size of a small house cat. It is usually a rich chocolate brown with a small white chin patch that is sometimes difficult to see. The body is long and slinky in appearance. Mink are about twenty to thirty inches long, including the tail, and weigh around two pounds. They live along streams and lakes and are abroad chiefly at night. They can be found in most parts of the country except sections of the Southwest.

MOLE A small, stout, burrowing animal with short legs, pointed nose, naked tail, and eyes so small as to be barely visible. A mole has oversized front feet, broader than they are long, with soles that turn outward. The fur, which is very soft and can be brushed in any direction, is brown or gray with a silvery sheen. Average length is six or seven inches, average weight two to four ounces. Moles like sandy loam in gardens, lawns, fields, meadows, and golf courses. The common mole is found throughout eastern and central United States. The western mole and shrew mole are found along the West Coast. The hairy-tailed and star-nosed moles are found in the East.

MOOSE The largest member of the deer family, the moose is an ungainly looking animal with humped shoulders, an overhanging snout, and a flap of skin on the throat resembling a bell. The moose is dark brown with paler brown legs. Males have heavy, flat antlers. Height at shoulders varies from five to seven and one-half feet. Males weigh from 850 pounds to 1,400 pounds, or even more in exceptional cases. Females are smaller. Moose are often found in or near the water, in coniferous forests of the northern states and in the Rocky Mountains.

MOUNTAIN GOAT, see **GOAT, MOUNTAIN**

MOUSE, WHITE-FOOTED Resembles a large house mouse, but underparts are pure white rather than gray. The upper parts are pale to rich reddish brown. White-footed mice have large eyes, long noses, big ears, and long, fairly hairy tails. They are five to ten inches long and weigh from one-half to one and three-fourths ounces. They prefer wooded or brushy areas. White-footed or deer mice (genus Peromyscus) are the most abundant mammals in North

America and can be found practically everywhere in the United States.

MUSKRAT A large brown water rat with hind feet that are partially webbed and are much longer than the front feet. The tail is long, black, scaly, nearly naked, and flattened from side to side. Eyes and ears are small. The fur is dense and "waterproofed" with oil. Total length is from seventeen to twenty-five inches, and weight is from two to four pounds. The muskrat is now the principal animal in the fur trade, and can be found in marshes, ponds, lakes, and streams nearly everywhere in the United States.

OPOSSUM A gray, bushy-furred marsupial about the size of a house cat. It has long, pointed nose, naked ears, short legs, and a long, naked tail, which is used to curl around objects. It is two and one-half to three feet in length and weighs eight to fifteen pounds. It prefers farming areas and woodlands, and is active only at night. It is found from the East Coast westward to Wisconsin, Colorado, and Texas, and also along the Pacific Coast. Its range appears to be spreading.

OTTER, RIVER An otter is a large weasel-like animal with fur that is rich brown above, silvery gray below. It has a flattened head, broad face, slender body, tapering tail, short legs, and webbed feet. Otters are three and one-half to four and one-half feet in length and weigh ten to twenty-five pounds. They are found along streams and lakes and are seldom seen on land, though in winter they may travel overland to seek waterfalls, rapids, or other bodies of water that do not freeze in cold weather. Otters are playful and fun to watch. They range throughout most of the United States but are very rare.

POCKET GOPHER, see **GOPHER, POCKET**

PORCUPINE This heavy-bodied, short-legged, clumsy animal with the arched back, small head, and heavy tail is easily recognized. It is the only North American mammal with long sharp quills. When the animal is not alarmed, the quills are almost hidden by blackish fur with numerous white-tipped hairs. When attacked, the porcupine raises its quills, making a pincushion of itself. It is quite a large animal, twenty-seven to forty inches in length, weighing ten to twenty-eight pounds or more. It is most active at night but may sometimes be seen during the day high in the trees. It is found in the Northeast, in the north central border states, in the western half of the United States, and in Alaska.

PRAIRIE DOG A rather large, plump rodent with a flattened head, small ears, and short tail. It is yellowish or cinnamon buff in color. Length is twelve to seventeen inches, weight one and one-half to three pounds. Prairie dogs, which are actually ground squirrels, get the last part of their name from their habit of barking. Black-tailed prairie dogs, which are the most common kind, live in colonies marked by bare mounds of earth around each dwelling hole. They are found in parks and in a few scattered western prairie areas, but most have been poisoned out of existence. The white-tailed variety, also rare, lives in valleys in the Rocky Mountains.

PREDATOR An animal that gets its food primarily by killing and consuming other animals.

PRONGHORN (ANTELOPE) A graceful, medium-sized hoofed mammal, easy to recognize by the two broad white bands across the throat and the dazzling white circle that appears on the rump when the animal is excited. Both sexes have single-forked horns, though the female's are smaller. The outer covering of the horns is shed annually. Pronghorns are about three feet tall at the shoulders and weigh 75 to 130 pounds. They are active in the daytime and are usually seen in small bands. They are found on the plains in dry areas of western United States.

RABBIT, COTTONTAIL Cottontails are medium-sized rabbits with ears and hind feet that are fairly long, but not so long as those of jack rabbits and other hares. The eastern cottontail is the most widespread and common species. Like most other cottontails, it has a tail with a white underside that looks like a ball of cotton when raised. Total length varies from eleven to twenty-two inches; weight is usually two to four pounds, but can be up to six pounds. Cottontails like brushy or swampy areas, weed patches, and gardens, and are active from early evening to late morning. One species or another of cottontail can be found almost everywhere in the United States.

RACCOON The raccoon is easy to recognize because of its black mask and the black rings on its tail. The general body color is salt and pepper. The raccoon is a bushy-haired, chunky animal that usually comes out only at night. Total length, including tail, is twenty-six to forty inches. The average weight runs from twelve to thirty-five pounds. Raccoons prefer to be along streams and lakes where there are wooded areas or rocky cliffs nearby. They sometimes come to suburban areas to raid garbage cans, and may become quite tame. They can be found almost everywhere in the United States.

RANGE   The region throughout which a kind of animal naturally lives.

RED FOX, see **FOX, RED**

RED SQUIRREL, see **SQUIRREL, RED**

RIVER OTTER, see **OTTER, RIVER**

RUT   A cycle in the life of a mammal when it is most fertile and most easily aroused sexually.

SHEEP, BIGHORN   This is a large, chunky sheep with brown horns. The male's horns are massive and curl back, out, and forward to almost a full circle; those of ewes and young males are only slightly curved. The coat of the bighorn is hairy rather than woolly. The color varies from grayish brown to blackish brown. A creamy white rump patch is a distinguishing characteristic. Height is two and one-half to three and one-half feet at the shoulder; weight is from 125 to 275 pounds. Females are smaller. Bighorns are rare, found only in the mountainous areas of western United States.

SKUNK   There are four kinds of skunks in the United States, the striped, the spotted, the hog-nosed, and the hooded skunk. The striped or common skunk, about the size of a house cat, is the most widespread. It is black with a white stripe on the forehead that branches out into two white stripes which run to the base of the tail. The bushy tail is usually black and white. Total length of striped skunks varies from twenty to thirty inches, weight from three and one-half to ten pounds.

SQUIRREL, FLYING   Flying squirrels are small tree squirrels that have soft, silky fur, large eyes, a flattened tail, and folded layers of loose skin that stretch between the front legs and the hind legs. These loose, furred "wings" enable the animal to glide. Because they are active only at night, flying squirrels are seldom seen. Fur color on the upper part of the body is brown, varying in shade and hue. The underparts are white. Length, including tail, is from nine to fourteen inches, weight from one and one-half to six ounces.

Eastern flying squirrels are found in the eastern half of the United States. Northern flying squirrels, which are larger, are found in many of the northern states, in the Appalachians as far south as Tennessee, in the western mountains, and along the Pacific Coast.

SQUIRREL, GRAY The most familiar of the squirrels, the eastern gray squirrel is a large tree squirrel with a very bushy tail, frosted with white, and rounded ears. The length, including the tail, varies from seventeen to twenty-three inches, and the weight averages three-fourths to one and one-half pounds. Gray squirrels are active during the daytime. They can be found in parks and suburban areas as well as in forests. Gray squirrels are easily tamed. They live in the eastern half of the United States, in the Pacific Coast states, and in parts of Arizona and New Mexico.

SQUIRREL, RED This is the smallest of the tree squirrels that are active in the daytime. It is rusty red above, white below. Its tail is bushy, but not so bushy as the gray squirrel's. It is eleven to fourteen inches in length and weighs five to ten and one-half ounces. It often announces its presence by a loud "scolding." The red squirrel prefers to nest in coniferous forests and gathers as its principal foods the seeds of spruce, fir, and pine. It ranges throughout most of the northern states, the Rocky Mountains, and the Appalachian region.

TIMBER WOLF, see **WOLF, EASTERN TIMBER**

WEAN To accustom young to take food other than by nursing.

WHITE-FOOTED MOUSE, see **MOUSE, WHITE-FOOTED**

WHITE-TAILED DEER, see **DEER, WHITE-TAILED**

WOLF, EASTERN TIMBER The largest of the wild dogs, the eastern timber wolf looks somewhat like an overgrown German shepherd. It is usually gray but may vary from nearly white to nearly black. It can be distinguished from a coyote by its larger size and by the fact that it carries its tail high when running, not low as a coyote does. Its legs are longer than those of a domestic dog, and its front legs are closer together because of its narrower chest. Its total length is four to seven feet; weight averages 70 to 120 pounds. Timber wolves were once abundant in the United States, but only Alaska and Minnesota have significant numbers today.

WOLF, MEXICAN   A very small, dark wolf, the smallest in North America, the Mexican wolf has a short face and wide cheeks. Males weigh about one hundred pounds, females about seventy pounds. They are found in extreme southern Arizona and Texas.

WOLF, NORTHERN ROCKY MOUNTAIN   This is a medium-sized to large wolf, generally light in color, with hair tips gray or black. It has been reported in Yellowstone and Glacier National Parks and in certain nearby national forests.

WOLF, RED   A slender, medium-sized wolf, the red wolf resembles a coyote but is larger, with longer legs and ears. Its fur may be black or may resemble that of the coyote. The red wolf is found only in Louisiana and eastern Texas.

WOODCHUCK   A large, heavy-bodied, short-tailed ground squirrel with brown fur that is often slightly "frosted" with white. It is also called a groundhog and is noted for its deep hibernation and its appearance or nonappearance on February 2. It is sixteen to twenty-five inches in total length; average weight is five to ten pounds. Woodchucks are found in open woods and brushy ravines in the eastern half of the United States, with the exception of some of the southern states.